God's Man

A Pastor's Handbook

World Evangelical Harvest

World Evangelical Harvest is a registered 501(C)3 Nonprofit Organization

www.worldeharvest.org

God's Man

A Pastor's Handbook

Paul D. LeFavor

Blacksmith Publishing

Fayetteville, North Carolina

"Return, O backsliding children," says the Lord; "for I am married to you. I will take you, one from a city and two from a family, and I will bring you to Zion. And I will give you shepherds according to My heart, who will feed you with knowledge and understanding" (Jer 3:14-15).

God's Man: A Pastor's Handbook
by Paul D. LeFavor

Library of Congress Number:

ISBN 978-1-7329681-3-4

Printed in the United States of America

Published by Blacksmith LLC
Fayetteville, NC

www.Blacksmithpublishing.com

Direct inquiries and/or orders to the above web address.

The Lord's Prayer

"After this manner therefore pray ye: Our Father which art in heaven, Hallowed be thy name. Thy kingdom come, Thy will be done in earth, as it is in heaven. Give us this day our daily bread. And forgive us our debts, as we forgive our debtors. And lead us not into temptation, but deliver us from evil: For thine is the kingdom, and the power, and the glory, for ever. Amen" (Mt 6:9-13).

For my fellow undershepherds.
Your labor is not in vain (1 Cor 15:58).

Contents

Part Four: Seven Core Directives

Part Five: Pastoral Resources

Preface

Jesus said, if you love Me, "Feed My lambs...tend my sheep...feed My sheep." – John 21:15, 16, 17.

C. S. Lewis once observed, "there are theologians in the bottom of hell who were more interested in their own thoughts about God than in God himself." It was for this reason, Lewis counseled, that a "dogmatician" should also preach regularly. Lewis' pithy observation underscores an immensely important point in the life of any preacher: One's walk with the Lord Jesus must not only be genuine, it must be vibrant. This is especially true for men who have consecrated themselves to the task of leading the Lord's people as an under shepherd – pastor. Preparing for the ministry begins by applying God's Word to oneself (1 Tim 4:16).

Moreover, men who serve as pastors in the church should be gifted to that end, and above all, they must have a mind for truth and a heart for God. In other words, above all other qualifications, a man must be born again and have received God's call and gifts to serve as pastor (Jn 3:3; Eph 4:11).

In addition to a calling, chief among the qualities a pastor should possess is wisdom. However, this attribute doesn't always come with age, and some can be wise beyond their years. If a pastor doesn't have wisdom, he should be wise enough to ask the Lord for it (Jam 1:5; 3:17; Pro 2:3-6). In addition to wisdom, pastoring requires prudence, that is, being able to assess given circumstances correctly and then act appropriately. Prudence may be best thought of as the handmaiden of wisdom. Prudence is knowing what to say and how to say it. But prudence is short changed without patience. So, what this looks like is: Wisdom assesses an issue that has become known, then prudence takes over as to how to address it, and patience moderates attitudes, actions and affections.

Added to all of these godly characteristics, a pastor must also possess thick skin, as potential "slights" abound. Putting all these qualities together, a pastor requires the wisdom of Solomon, the prudence of Jethro, the patience of Job, and the hide of a rhinoceros. Moreover, these qualities must be undergirded by the humility and love of Christ. Possessing these and having a mind for truth and love for God and mankind, a pastor must be truly called and know it, God gifted, and motivated to serve as Christ's undershepherd. That is quite a lot! What this therefore brings to mind is a pastor is a man who understands God's grace and is in ready need of it.

A pastor is also to be a theologian, as theology is the study of God as well as the application of His Word to all areas of life. This is essentially the purpose for this pastor's handbook, to provide a simple resource to encapsulate the most important truths of our common salvation, to equip pastors for the work of ministering the Word. For assuredly, what the Church most desperately needs to recover is sound biblical teaching and preaching that is deliberately Trinitarian, highly Christocentric, and urgently evangelistic. It is my prayer that this book represents a prescription for the Church's present need.

Pastor Paul D. LeFavor
Christ Covenant Baptist Church
Easter 2019

Introduction

"So he shepherded them according to the integrity of his heart, and guided them by the skillfulness of his hands."
– Psalm 78:72

Has God called you into the ministry? If you feel He has, let me begin by saying that within Christ's 'general calling' to be His servants, is a 'particular calling' to serve Him as minister of the Word. And so, it has been rightly said, the nature of one's ministry is determined by the gift received. When God calls a man to be a pastor, He calls him to witness the saving truths of the gospel of Jesus Christ and to lead one of His congregations as an undershepherd. This calling is to equip His "saints for the work of ministry, for the edifying (literally, building up) of the body of Christ" (Eph 4:12-14).

Every pastor should take his calling seriously. For you serve the Lord Christ (Col 3:24). For as Charles H. Spurgeon has aptly stated, "No one may intrude into the sheepfold as an undershepherd; he must have an eye to the chief Shepherd, and await His beck and command."[1] Likewise, in the parable of the places of honor at the table, Jesus teaches that we are not to presume to take a choice seat but rather to humbly wait for the King to call us forward to serve Him (Lk 14:14).

Moreover, if you are called by the Lord, that calling will be confirmed by God's people, who, sensing the wisdom and guidance of the Holy Spirit, will call upon you to serve as Christ's undershepherd. For, assuredly, the scriptural calling comes not only through the heart

---

[1] Charles H. Spurgeon, *Lectures to My Students* (Peabody, MA: Hendrickson, 2011), 25.

of the candidate, but also from the Church itself. In other words, the call is never complete until the church has confirmed it. "Those who profess to be called of God," writes Spurgeon, are "selected to their positions by the free choice of believers."[2]

Therefore, it may truly be said that the call comes from God through His people. The sheep must hear the voice of the Shepherd through the undershepherd. Along with the candidate's aptitude for preaching, and consent of the flock, Spurgeon writes, "That which finally evidences a proper call, is a correspondent opening in providence, by a gradual train of circumstances pointing out the means, the time, the place of actually entering upon the work."[3]

Considering all of this, every pastor should take his calling very seriously. First, because being called to pastor is being called to die. It's a call to follow Jesus and imitate His life and ministry, to take up your cross daily, to mediate God's truth and grace to a rebellious world groaning under the weight of its sin. Second, if you are married, it means serving Christ as a faithful family man, to love and honor your wife and children that God has called you to lead. Your family of course will be an example to the flock. Third, it means serving Christ as the leader of a congregation: By providing purpose, direction and motivation to a congregation; by faithfully preaching and teaching God's Holy Word; by loving the people, caring for their needs, and protecting them from dangerous influences.

If you are called of the Lord, be well aware that this is a high and holy calling. Without this defining

---

[2] Ibid., 85.
[3] Ibid., 36.

characteristic of the call, the intruder will be found guilty of the sin of Uzzah. He was wrong in presuming to serve God in a way that God had not prescribed (2 Sam 6:6-8). In the Book of Jeremiah, the genuine call is demonstrated over against the presumptuous when God says,

> "I have not sent these prophets, yet they ran. I have not spoken to them, yet they prophesied. But if they had stood in My counsel, and had caused My people to hear My words, then they would have turned them from their evil way and from the evil of their doings" (Jer 23:21-22).

All are not called to labor in the Word and doctrine but if a man desires the position of an elder, he desires a good work (1 Tim 3:1).

It is clearly evident to us from Scripture that Christ Himself gifts and calls men to serve His church (Eph 4:11). It is through these appointed officers that Christ governs His church. In light of all this, how do we know if we are called? You must have an intense, all-absorbing desire for the work. You must feel, "woe unto me for I must preach the gospel," as Isaiah, Jeremiah and Ezekiel did (Is 6:8; Jer 20:9; Ezek 2:1-3). How can we justify our calling if we don't have a similar call (Acts 20:17-32)? If you are called of God to preach the Word, the passion will bear the test of time. Christ's gifts will confirm your calling. What God requires: He gives.

As God's men, we are called to be His office bearers. We are called and equipped to shepherd His flock which He purchased with His own blood (Acts 20). We stand like watchman on the walls and preach the King's degree. We are called to be faithful to God's message.

We are called to call others to repentance and faith. We are called to pronounce God's judgments along with the promise of His forgiveness to those who repent and believe in Jesus Christ. Perhaps most of all, we are called to love others and suffer long with them. And like God's men of old, we are called to persevere in troubles, while our message is often largely ignored.

The purpose of this book is to bring glory to God by equipping pastors with tools for shepherding God's people. The God-given role of the pastor may be understood to be threefold. To serve the Lord Jesus as His undershepherd by: **Guiding**, **providing** and **protecting** Christ's sheep. Expounding upon these three roles, a pastor serves Christ by: (1) *Leading* the church in disciple-making (Mt 28:18-20); (2) *Gathering, equipping and edifying* the saints through preaching and teaching the Word of God (Eph 4:11-16); and (3) *Protecting* the flock with nurturing care (1 Pet 5:2-3). See diagram below.

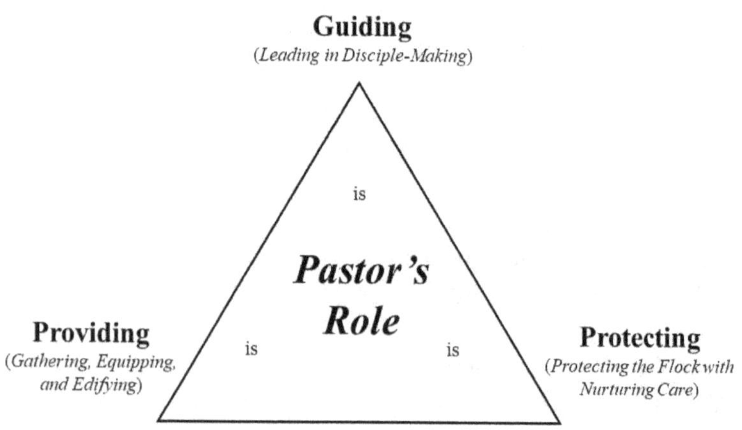

Pastor's Three-fold Role.

The goal of this book will be to flesh out this threefold role of pastoral ministry. With this aim, this book is divided into five parts. Part one identifies Christ's mission as Good Shepherd and the purpose and role of His undershepherds. Part two surveys the principle doctrines of the Christian faith that God's man should preach and teach. Parts three and four lays out both the doctrinal and practical aspects of the ministry. Finally, part five provides pastoral resources.

Pastoring is the greatest calling and privilege. A pastor is God's man. He is called to shepherd the flock put under his care according to God's heart. He is called to feed God's people with God's word (Jer 3:14-15). If what I have written equips you with tools for serving Christ as His undershepherd, my purpose has been attained. Soli Deo Gloria.

Part One: God's Man

The mission of the pastor is to serve the Lord Jesus as His undershepherd (Jn 21:15-19) by: Leading the church in disciple-making (Mt 28:18-20; 2 Tim 2:1-2); gathering-equipping-edifying through preaching and teaching of the Word of God (Acts 20:20-28; Eph 4:11-16; 2 Tim 4:1-5); while protecting the flock with nurturing care (Acts 20:29-32; 1 Pet 5:2-3).

Chapter One: The Shepherd of Israel

"Sheep may safely graze and pasture when their Shepherd guards them well." – Johann Sebastian Bach

The Bible is about God and His relationship to humanity. In the Old Testament, one of the principle metaphors God uses for Himself is the Shepherd of Israel (Ps 80:1). In fact, the whole history of God's people can be traced using the metaphor of God as the shepherd of his people. From the exodus from Egypt, to the second exodus from the wilderness of this world, God is the Shepherd of his people. Likewise, God's people are "the sheep of His pasture" (Ps 95:7; 100:3).

Jacob refers to God in this sense when he says: "The God who has fed רָעָה *rah ah* (shepherded) me all my life long to this day" (Gen 48:15). What Jacob meant was God is the Shepherd of His people as He guides them to green pastures, provides for their needs and protects them from harm. God promised to always be with His people to Shepherd them to ensure the fulfillment of His promises to Abraham.

In the account of the Exodus, shepherd terminology is used to describe God's leading of His people. For example, the Psalmist, describing God's shepherding of the entire nation of Israel through the Exodus, writes: "You led Your people like a flock by the hand of Moses and Aaron" (Ps 77:20). Psalm 78:51-53 declares: The Lord "destroyed all the firstborn in Egypt, the first of their strength in the tents of Ham. But He made His own people go forth like sheep, and guided them in the wilderness like a flock; and He led them on safely, so that they did not fear."

As the Exodus account demonstrates, with a strong arm, God delivered His people out of Egypt and brought them to Mount Zion. God appointed various servants "to shepherd Jacob His people, and Israel His inheritance" (Ps 78:71). David "shepherded them according to the integrity of his heart, and guided them by the skillfulness of his hands" (Ps 78:72). As Israel's undershepherd, David famously extolled the shepherding care of God in Psalm 23:

> The Lord is my shepherd; I shall not want. 2 He makes me to lie down in green pastures; He leads me beside the still waters. 3 He restores my soul; He leads me in the paths of righteousness for His name's sake. 4 Yea, though I walk through the valley of the shadow of death, I will fear no evil; For You are with me; Your rod and Your staff, they comfort me. 5 You prepare a table before me in the presence of my enemies; You anoint my head with oil; my cup runs over. 6 Surely goodness and mercy shall follow me all the days of my life; and I will dwell in the house of the Lord forever.

Psalm 23 describes God's shepherding care in essentially three ways: His ***guidance*** (verses 2 and 3), ***provision*** (verses 1 and 5) and **protection** (verses 2, 4, 5, and 6). The Lord guides, provides and protects His sheep. In fact, the whole history of Israel is described as one pastoral journey. From the days of Jacob, through the exodus under Moses, to the possession of the Promised Land under Joshua, God relates to his people as their Shepherd (Ps 23:1).

The Scriptures also tell the story of how Israel became unfaithful to God because they were led by irresponsible shepherds (Ezek 34:1-10). As a result of their unfaithfulness to the covenant, the people were scattered into exile (Lev 26:33). Looking past the nation's exile, the prophet Isaiah saw a second exodus. This would be an exodus out of slavery to Satan and sin and into the holiness of the new creation:

> Behold, the Lord God shall come with a strong hand, and His arm shall rule for Him; behold, His reward is with Him, and His work before Him. He will feed His flock like a shepherd; He will gather the lambs with His arm, and carry them in His bosom, and gently lead those who are with young (Is 40:10-11).

Likewise, Jeremiah foresaw the same thing and declared:

> Hear the word of the Lord, O nations, and declare it in the isles afar off, and say, 'He who scattered Israel will gather him, and keep him as a shepherd does his flock.' For the Lord has redeemed Jacob, and ransomed him from the hand of one stronger than he. Therefore they shall come and sing in the height of Zion, streaming to the goodness of the Lord— For wheat and new wine and oil, for the young of the flock and the herd; their souls shall be like a well-watered garden, and they shall sorrow no more at all (Jer 31:10-12).

In Jeremiah's day, the shepherds of the people were stupid and selfish, leading to the flock being scattered. Through Jeremiah, God promised to give His people new shepherds:

> "Return, O backsliding children," says the Lord; "for I am married to you. I will take you, one from a city and two from a family, and I will bring you to Zion.

> And I will give you shepherds according to My heart, who will feed you with knowledge and understanding (Jer 3:14-15).

These new shepherds promised by God will be gifts to the people. They will be shepherds who share God's heart for His sheep. They will nourish and sustain God's sheep with knowledge and understanding.

Micah, a contemporary of Isaiah, also prophesied God's gathering His sheep from exile:

> I will surely assemble all of you, O Jacob, I will surely gather the remnant of Israel; I will put them together like sheep of the fold, like a flock in the midst of their pasture; they shall make a loud noise because of so many people. The one who breaks open will come up before them; They will break out, pass through the gate, and go out by it; their king will pass before them, with the Lord at their head (Mic 2:12-13).

After the people went into captivity, through the prophet Ezekiel, God announced He would raise up a Shepherd over His people: "I will establish one shepherd over them, and he shall feed them—My servant David. He shall feed them and be their shepherd" (Ezek 34:23). As this prophecy announces, it is in the regathering of His flock in which God reestablishes Israel.

This prophecy was partially fulfilled when God restored his people to the Promised Land under Zerubbabel, Ezra and Nehemiah. However, the prophecy telegraphs further into the future because it is said that "David" would be the shepherd. Rather than being a resurrected David, this prophecy refers to the Son of David, Jesus Christ (Mt 1:1).

It is therefore in the advent of the Son of God that Ezekiel's prophecy finds its ultimate fulfillment as Jesus the Good Shepherd began to reestablish the nucleus of restored Israel in His disciples. It is through undershepherds that Christ gathers the remnant of His flock as Jeremiah prophesied: "I will set up shepherds over them who will feed them; and they shall fear no more, nor be dismayed, nor shall they be lacking" (Jer 23:4). As we study the whole Bible what we find is the whole cannon of Scripture testifies that Jesus Christ is the Good Shepherd and the Shepherd of Israel.

The Good Shepherd

By the time of the earthly ministry of Jesus, the Old Testament religion of grace lived by Abraham and the patriarchs had degenerated into a rigid, external, legalistic, works righteousness. Led by the Pharisees, the people lifted the law out of its gracious roots, all the while preserving the external practices of worship without its essential heart. John chapter nine demonstrates the bad shepherding of the Pharisees after Jesus heals a man born blind. The Pharisees abused and mistreated this man and cast him out (Jn 9:34; cf. Ezek 34:1-10). Over against this mistreatment, using the shepherd metaphor, Jesus declares Himself the Good Shepherd who will care for God's people.

Jesus first warns of false shepherds that intrude into the sheepfold of God to take advantage of the people and profit from their expense (Jn 10:1). As "thieves and robbers," they steal what belongs to God and "fleece" the flock, attempt to take what belongs to God. These false shepherds are those who wear sheep's clothing but are really "ravenous wolves" (Mt 7:15). They teach traditions rather than God's Word (Mt 15:6). These false shepherds actually try to prevent people from entering the kingdom of heaven (Mt 23:13). They even pervert justice and murder God's people (Mt 5:11-12).

Jesus is the Good Shepherd. Shepherding God's people is His mission. Jesus declares from the beginning that a true undershepherd of His is one who gains access to the sheep in the Divinely-appointed way. Unlike the Pharisees, who are referred to as thieves and robbers, a true undershepherd doesn't intrude himself into the sacred office, but is called to it by God (Jn 10:1).

To the true undershepherd, the "doorkeeper opens," that is the Holy Spirit sets before him an open door for ministry and service. As the divinely appointed undershepherd, the sheep hear his voice (Jn 10:3). Through His undershepherds Christ calls His own sheep by name and leads them out into the green pastures of God's Word where they may find food and rest. Of His mission Jesus says in John 10:11-18:

> 11 **"I am the good shepherd. The good**
> **shepherd gives His life for the sheep.** 12 But a
> hireling, he who is not the shepherd, one who does
> not own the sheep, sees the wolf coming and leaves
> the sheep and flees; and the wolf catches the sheep
> and scatters them. 13 The hireling flees because he is
> a hireling and does not care about the sheep. 14 **I am**
> **the good shepherd; and I know My sheep,**
> **and am known by My own.** 15 As the Father
> knows Me, even so I know the Father; and I lay down
> My life for the sheep. 16 And other sheep I have
> which are not of this fold; them also I must bring,
> and they will hear My voice; **and there will be one**
> **flock and one shepherd** (emphasis added).

In contrast to the hired hand (hireling), the good shepherd is so concerned for His sheep, He's willing to lay down His life for them. He's not afraid to sacrifice Himself for their good. He sacrifices Himself to protect His sheep from wolves.

Unlike the false shepherds and the hireling, He knows his sheep, calls them each by name and they follow Him willingly. He gathers His flock together and keeps them together. Notice there is one flock and one Shepherd, not two flocks. There is only one people of God that consists of people from every nation, tribe and tongue (Rev 7:9).

Jesus never referred to Himself as bishop, elder or preacher but He did refer to Himself as Shepherd. Leaving His undershepherds a godly example, directing them to do nothing that He is not able or willing to do himself. The good Shepherd dies for His sheep (Jn 10:11). Now, through His undershepherds, Christ guides, provides and protects His sheep.

Chapter Two: The Undershepherd

"Return, O backsliding children," says the Lord; "for I am married to you. I will take you, one from a city and two from a family, and I will bring you to Zion. 15 And I will give you shepherds according to My heart, who will feed you with knowledge and understanding (Jer 3:14-15)."

As we have seen, the shepherding metaphor is used to tell the story of how God guides, provides and protects His people. The shepherd metaphor is used to describe God's work and the work of his Son in the Old and New Testaments. The shepherd metaphor is also used to describe the men God specifically delegates to represent Him in His work of shepherding His people.

In the last chapter of John's Gospel, Jesus stands Peter back up on his apostolic feet. Having restored Peter, Jesus conveys to him the task of shepherding. Jesus teaches Peter that He will be accomplishing His mission through him:

> 15 So when they had eaten breakfast, Jesus said to
> Simon Peter, "Simon, son of Jonah, do you love Me
> more than these?" He said to Him, "Yes, Lord; You
> know that I love You." He said to him, "Feed My
> lambs." 16 He said to him again a second time,
> "Simon, son of Jonah, do you love Me?" He said to
> Him, "Yes, Lord; You know that I love You." He said
> to him, "Tend My sheep." 17 He said to him the third
> time, "Simon, son of Jonah, do you love Me?" Peter
> was grieved because He said to him the third time,
> "Do you love Me?" And he said to Him, "Lord, You
> know all things; You know that I love You." Jesus
> said to him, "Feed My sheep. 18 Most assuredly, I say

> to you, when you were younger, you girded yourself and walked where you wished; but when you are old, you will stretch out your hands, and another will gird you and carry you where you do not wish." 19 This He spoke, signifying by what death he would glorify God. And when He had spoken this, He said to him, "Follow Me" (Jn 21:15-19).

Christ's mission to Peter is as moving as it is instructive. It conveys to us four key truths:

First, our love for Jesus is demonstrated by feeding His sheep. Jesus said to Simon Peter, if you love Me "feed My lambs" (Jn 21:15). A pastor is an undershepherd of Jesus Christ. A pastor is a man whom the Lord raises up to care for the total well-being of His flock (the people of God). The sheep aren't his. Rather they belong to Jesus. They're His sheep. Christ's first concern for His sheep is that they are fed with His Word: "Feed My lambs."

Looking again at John 21, by using the term "lambs" evidently Jesus meant newborn Christians. In this vein, exhorting believers in his first letter, Peter writes "as newborn babes, desire the pure milk of the word, that you may grow" (1 Pet 2:1). This teaches us all about the role of God's Word in the life of the one He has caused to be born again. A chief part of the role of pastor is to guide Christ's lambs into all truth, feeding them with the Word of God through preaching, teaching, and modeling the Christian life.

Second, our shepherding care is our stewarding of those who belong to Jesus. Jesus said to him again a second time, "Simon, son of Jonah, do you love Me?" He said to Him, "Yes, Lord; You know that I love You." He said to him, "Tend My sheep" (Jn 21:16). Tending Christ's sheep involves equipping and edifying them. It means helping them discover their gifts and enabling them to step out in faith to use them. This involves oversight and patience, bearing up with their faults.

Third, our care for Christ's sheep will cause us to suffer, following Christ's example. Jesus said to him the third time, "Simon, son of Jonah, do you love Me?" Jesus said to him, "Feed My sheep. Most assuredly, I say to you, when you were younger, you girded yourself and walked where you wished; but when you are old, you will stretch out your hands, and another will gird you and carry you where you do not wish." This He spoke, signifying by what death he would glorify God. And when He had spoken this, He said to him, "Follow Me" (Jn 21:17-19).

This teaches that a pastor's purpose is to lead God's people in disciple-making, demonstrating what a life of sacrifice for Christ looks like. Jesus said that every disciple when fully trained will be like Him (Lk 6:40; cf. 1 Cor 11:1). Jesus teaches us when we follow His example and feed His sheep it will cause us to suffer.

Peter was also curious as to what the Lord would do with John and so he asked Jesus: "Lord, what about this man?" And Jesus replied, "If I will that he remain till I come, what is that to you?" You follow Me" (Jn 21:22). In other words, Jesus says we aren't to compare our calling with someone else's calling.

Above all, a pastor's mission is to embrace the Great Commission (Mt 28:18-20). As such, a pastor is called to make disciples who make disciples through a process of disciple-making that involves worship, preaching and teaching, nurturing, and protecting. A pastor is a disciple-maker who is to exhort disciples to make disciples (2 Tim 2:2).

The Apostle Peter never forgot these words of Jesus, and writing in his first epistle, he declares much regarding the undershepherd's heart. Looking again at 1 Pet 5:2, Peter declares:

> The elders who are among you I exhort, I who am a fellow elder and a witness of the sufferings of Christ, and also a partaker of the glory that will be revealed: 2 Shepherd the flock of God which is among you, serving as overseers, not by compulsion but willingly, not for dishonest gain but eagerly; 3 nor as being lords over those entrusted to you, but being examples to the flock; 4 and when the Chief Shepherd appears, you will receive the crown of glory that does not fade away (1 Peter 5:2-4).

This passage follows on the heels of a chapter steeped in Peter's exhortation to make oneself ready for persecution. His point is: When God's people face fiery trials, the first to do so are always the elders and leaders of God's people. And history shows us that is precisely what has happened for the last twenty centuries. When persecution comes, the leadership is always targeted first. In other words, because judgment begins at the house of God, it especially begins with the elders and leaders. Peter therefore sees a special need to exhort the elders in view of the fiery ordeal that is coming.

By this name "elders" he designates pastors and all those who are appointed for the government of the Church. This raises an important point. The word "pastor," in the Greek is ποιμήν *poimen*, means a shepherd. In Latin the word is pastor. The Apostle Paul tells us "If a man desires the position of a bishop (elder), he desires a good work" (1 Tim 3:1). The terms elder, pastor, and over-seer (translated bishop or presbyter) refer to the same office. Some consider the office of elder to be the same as "pastor," while others choose a group of men to serve as presbyters (session), often with the lead elder (preaching elder) ministering the Word and ordinances. In 1 Peter 5:1-2, the apostle Peter brings all three of these terms together. The point is, these terms are used to describe various aspects of the same ministry.

Then, in verse 2, when he writes "Shepherd the flock of God which is among you by exercising oversight," he means you are to actually know those you are responsible for. This is why he adds "as overseers." That is, those souls entrusted to you. One's motivation and attitude in this regard is very important. And so, he adds, shepherd them not because you feel you have to but because you want to. Our goal in all of this is also important. Likewise, he adds, shepherd not for personal gain either but for God's glory. Moreover, we should always bear in mind these are Christ's sheep. Therefore, we are to shepherd not as lords but rather as servants (1 Pet 5:3).

Lastly, in verse 4, Peter admonishes pastors to shepherd in light of the Chief Shepherd's return (cf. 2 Tim 4:1). In a pattern of words that is reminiscent of Christ's parable of the faithful servant and evil servant, Peter underscores the words of Jesus "for everyone to whom much is given, from him much will be required" (Lk 12:48). In light of Christ's return to judge the living and the dead, Peter exhorts pastors to minister faithfully and urgently. The pastoral ministry is an urgent ministry, Jesus Christ will return soon to judge the living and the dead (2 Tim 4:1).

The Tasks of the Undershepherd

The undershepherd is God's Man. We have seen the purpose (John 21) and the heart (1 Peter 5) of the undershepherd. As we come to the Book of Acts, the Apostle Paul teaches us the tasks of the undershepherd. In Acts 20, the Apostle Paul is on his way to Jerusalem, and as his ship halts in Miletus he calls for the elders of the church in Ephesus. And when they had come to him, he said:

> "You know, from the first day that I came to Asia, in
> what manner I always lived among you, 19 ***serving***
> the Lord with all humility, with many tears and trials
> which happened to me by the plotting of the Jews;
> 20 how I ***kept back nothing that was helpful***,
> but proclaimed it to you, and ***taught you*** publicly
> and from house to house, 21 ***testifying*** to Jews, and
> also to Greeks, repentance toward God and faith
> toward our Lord Jesus Christ. 22 And see, now I go
> bound in the spirit to Jerusalem, not knowing the
> things that will happen to me there, 23 except that
> the Holy Spirit testifies in every city, saying that
> ***chains and tribulations await me***. 24 But none
> of these things move me; nor do I count my life dear
> to myself, ***so that I may finish my race with
> joy***, and the ministry which I received from the Lord
> Jesus, to testify to the gospel of the grace of God. 25
> "And indeed, now I know that you all, among whom
> I have gone preaching the kingdom of God, will see
> my face no more. 26 Therefore I testify to you this
> day that I am innocent of the blood of all men. 27
> ***For I have not shunned to declare to you the
> whole counsel of God***. 28 Therefore ***take heed
> to yourselves and to all the flock***, among which
> the Holy Spirit has made you overseers, to

> ***shepherd the church of God which He purchased with His own blood.*** 29 For I know this, that after my departure savage wolves will come in among you, not sparing the flock. 30 Also from among yourselves men will rise up, speaking perverse things, to draw away the disciples after themselves. 31 Therefore watch, and remember that for three years I did not cease to warn everyone night and day with tears. 32 "So now, brethren, I commend you to God and to the word of His grace, which is able to build you up and give you an inheritance among all those who are sanctified (Acts 20:18-32, emphasis added).

The apostle mentions at least ten major tasks here: First, Paul teaches us, as we shepherd (pastor) the flock, of which the Holy Spirit has made us overseers, we are to do so with the mindset that all service is rendered to the Lord Jesus (Acts 20:19). At all times a pastor is to remember he is an undershepherd of Jesus Christ. A pastor shepherds Christ's sheep. Second, the way we are to shepherd is by holding nothing back (Acts 20:20). In fact, when we have done our very best, that is only what we are supposed to do. Jesus makes these first two points in Luke 17:7-10:

> 7 And which of you, having a servant plowing or tending sheep, will say to him when he has come in from the field, 'Come at once and sit down to eat'? 8 But will he not rather say to him, 'Prepare something for my supper, and gird yourself and serve me till I have eaten and drunk, and afterward you will eat and drink'? 9 Does he thank that servant because he did the things that were commanded him? I think not. 10 So likewise you, when you have done all those things which you are commanded, say, 'We are

unprofitable servants. We have done what was our duty to do.'"

Third, we are to shepherd by teaching the Word of God publicly and from house to house (Acts 20:20). The sheep are to be fed God's Word not our philosophy. So many congregations are full of sheep who don't know God's Word because their pastors aren't teaching them. Can such shepherds really be called faithful?

Fourth, we are to shepherd by testifying to the gospel of grace (Acts 20:24). Pastors are to concern themselves with those outside as well as those within. Pastors are to do the work of an evangelist (2 Tim 4:5). As Christ's message to the church at Ephesus reminds us, you can have great doctrine but leave your first love (Rev 2:4). Jesus says demonstrate your love for Me by loving the lost and reaching them with the gospel. It's easy to blast people with the truth but not love them. Jesus hates sinful practices but loves sinners and died for them. What we are to do is love people enough to share Jesus with them. Pastors are to lead their congregations in evangelizing others, making disciples who make disciples.

Paul wrote "All who desire to live godly in Christ Jesus will suffer persecution" (2 Tim 3:11). Fifth, likewise, God's man must therefore be prepared to suffer, and "endure all things for the sake of the elect, that they may also obtain the salvation which is in Christ Jesus with eternal glory" (2 Tim 2:10). Just as the apostles suffered as they served the Lord, so will all true ministers of the gospel (Mt 5:10).

Sixth, the Apostle Paul envisioned his entire life and ministry to be like that of a race. The track he was to run was laid out especially for him, his job was to find it and finish it (Acts 16:6). Likewise, we are to run the race laid out before us and complete it in the strength the Lord supplies (2 Tim 4:7).

Seventh, we are to shepherd by preaching the kingdom of God to the extent that we will declare the whole counsel of God (Acts 20:25, 27). As a kingdom of priests, we embody the reign of Christ, mediating Christ's priestly and royal authority to the world by overcoming. We are to declare all of God's truth so that we will be found innocent of the blood of everyone we preach to. For his motivation in doing this, Paul drew from Ezekiel 33:1-7 which is God's command for His watchmen to urgently, faithfully and fully declare God's Word.

Eighth, we are to shepherd by taking heed to ourselves (Acts 20:28). A pastor is called to lead God's people in disciple-making, demonstrating what a life of sacrifice for Christ looks like. Jesus said that every disciple when fully trained will be like Him (Lk 6:40). Later, Paul gives this same exhortation to Timothy: "Take heed to yourself and to the doctrine." In other words, be careful not to disqualify yourself from the ministry. Practice what you preach. Having correct doctrine is paramount because you will live out what you believe.

Ninth, likewise, we are to shepherd by taking heed to the flock under our care (Acts 20:28). God purchased this flock with His own blood. Pastors are called to exercise oversight over those entrusted to their care. This means we need to work hard at knowing the sheep and making sure they know us. Pastors have to know who they are responsible for. Being a good undershepherd involves being engaged with God's people as much as possible. Some are better at this than others, and pastoral oversight will look different from shepherd to shepherd but we all need to work hard at knowing Christ's sheep. "Take heed to yourself and to the doctrine. Continue in them, for in doing this you will save both yourself and those who hear you" (1 Tim 4:16).

As we've noted, overemphasizing doctrinal purity may lead to a lack of concern for the outside world. However, a deemphasizing of doctrinal purity may lead to an over identification with the world. With this in mind, tenth, we are to shepherd by watching, that is staying spiritually awake (Acts 20:31). As pastors, we are called to remain vigilant to guard the flock. We must be on the lookout for wolves. We must protect the flock from false doctrine and practice. Likewise, we must not water down biblical doctrines in order to present a less offensive, more tolerating gospel. The Gospel is a sword (Heb 4:12)! As Charles Spurgeon once observed, "It's the whole business of the whole church to preach the whole gospel to the whole world."

Part Two: Seven Core Doctrines

There are fundamental doctrines of the Christian faith which serve to define Christianity. The principle task of a pastor is to preach and teach God's Word. This is the principle way in which he will fulfill his purpose of "equipping the saints for the work of ministry, for the edifying (literally, building up) the body of Christ" (Eph 4:12). The goal in part two will be to outline the traditional doctrines of the Christian faith: Holy Scripture, God, Man, Christ and the Holy Spirit, salvation, the Church, and the future or last things.

Chapter Three: Doctrine of Holy Scripture

"The recognition of the Bible as the special revelation of God depends on the conviction that its authors were inspired by the Holy Spirit." – Louis Berkhof

The Apostle Paul exhorted Timothy to watch his life and doctrine closely. This underscores the fact that a pastor can model Christ well to others but if he isn't preaching and teaching doctrine, the lambs won't grow into sheep (Jn 21:15). Moreover, preaching and teaching is to be framed by doctrine so as to encapsulate the most important truths of our common salvation. What is to be preached and taught therefore is the Bible and not the pastor's philosophy on life. With this as a must, it is therefore incumbent on the pastor to have a correct view of the Word of God. In this chapter, the goal is to demonstrate that the Bible is inspired, sufficient, and authoritative (See figure 3-1).

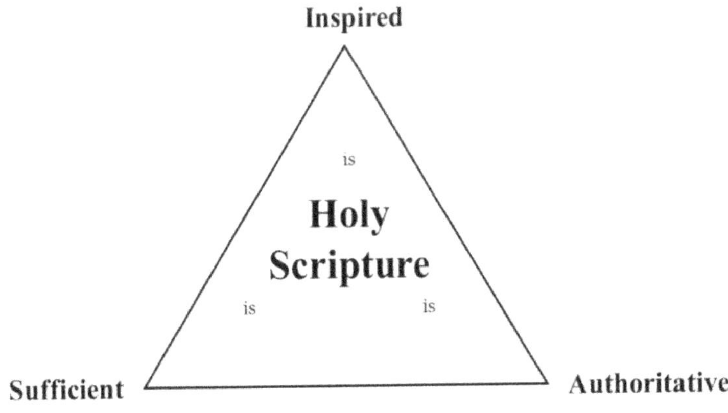

Figure 3-1. The Holy Scriptures.

Inspired – The Bible is a collection of documents that were written over a period of over 1,500 years on three continents, in three languages, by over forty authors, who wrote sixty-six volumes, that address hundreds of different topics which tells one redemptive story. The sixty-six Books that form the canon of the Old and New Testaments are divinely inspired and free from any error in the whole and in the part. These Books are given by inspiration of God, constitute His written word, and are the only infallible rule of faith and practice (2 Tim 3:16-17). Inspiration therefore means that every word of the Bible is "God-breathed" and that the choices of these words by human authors were under the superintendence of the Holy Spirit. The words of Scripture are not infallible due to the holiness of the human authors but because the Holy Spirit's superintendence.

Scripture is also the progressive self-revelation of God to His covenant people. As a living oracle, the Bible has been divinely composed through inspired human agency and preserved providentially in order to be heard and received by God's elect in all ages for all time. God moved men to write His words in such a way that the authors retained their cultural and linguistic patterns as well as their individuality, yet without the corruption of sin.

For this reason, the Scriptures are directly binding on the conscience, especially to those who have been regenerated and illuminated by God. By this pattern of sound words, the Holy Spirit actuates faith through truths that are requisite unto salvation for all whom Christ has purchased redemption.

Sufficient – The whole counsel of God concerning all things necessary for His own glory, man's salvation, faith and life, is either expressly set down in Scripture, or by good and necessary consequence may be deduced from Scripture; unto which nothing at any time is to be added, whether by new revelations of the Spirit, or traditions of men (Dt 12:32; Rev 22:18-19). Nevertheless, the inward illumination of the Spirit of God is necessary for the saving understanding of such things as are revealed in the Word. Moreover, there are some circumstances concerning the worship of God, and government of the Church, common to human actions and societies, which are to be ordered by the light of nature, and Christian prudence, according to the general rules of the Word, which are always to be observed.

Authoritative – The Bible alone is the Word of God and the only infallible rule of faith and practice. For this reason, the Scriptures are directly binding on the conscience, especially to those who have been regenerated and illuminated by God the Holy Spirit. By the inward illumination of the Spirit, the Scripture leads the Christian into all truth and authoritatively judges every thought and intention (Heb 4:12).

The final authority for the Christian is Scripture because it is the very Word of God. This doctrine is known as *sola Scriptura*, which in Latin means Scripture alone. Scripture is directly binding on conscience. To go against conscience is "neither right nor safe."

The Bible is not only inspired, sufficient, and authoritative, it is perfect and complete. This view is known as biblical inerrancy. Biblical inerrancy undergirds the fact that the Bible is the revelation of God's mind and will written by men, who, under the influence and guidance of the Holy Spirit, wrote God's very words. Benjamin Warfield once commented on how critical this doctrine was by observing:

> Failing to espouse this view of Scripture can destroy all Biblical doctrines, because a low view of Scripture undermines our confidence in the trustworthiness of Scripture as a witness to doctrine.[4]

The term used to describe the Bible's perfection is "plenary," derived from the Latin *plenus* meaning full and complete in every respect. Putting all these important terms together, plenary inspiration therefore serves as a "column" which buttresses the overarching "roof" of Biblical inerrancy. Along with the other columns of verbal inspiration, authority and sufficiency, these truths form a colonnade. If one were to remove any of these buttressing columns, the roof of Biblical inerrancy – along with the assurance with which it carries – collapses.

Plenary inspiration has been attacked from the beginning. As the apostolic writings were being circulated, even before the canon was compiled, men such as Marcion and a horde of other textual critics, plied their trade of operating on the original manuscripts or sometimes wrote their own.[5] These men rejected plenary inspiration. They denied the unity of the whole of Scripture by viewing certain authors as uninspired. They viewed the words of Jesus as inspired while rejecting the words of some or all the apostles.

---

[4] Benjamin B. Warfield, *The Inspiration and Authority of the Bible* (Philipsburg, NJ: P&R, 1980), 174.
[5] Eric F. Osborn, *Tertullian, The First Theologian of the West* (Peabody: Prince Press), 89.

Some even introduced spurious additions or made serious omissions to the gospels and to the apostle's epistles even in Peter's day. Peter writes about those who altered Paul's writings as they do the other Scriptures (2 Pet 3:16). Peter in this way acknowledges Paul's writings as equal to the Old Testament canon. The word "canon" comes from the Greek κανών, meaning "rule." The canon itself is its own ultimate authority and not an external source. In other words, the internal testimony of the Holy Spirit enables the church to see the canon for what it is. We can know which books belong in the canon because God works in the witness of the church to recognize the qualities that are there.[6]

Additionally, the doctrine of verbal inspiration has been denied on the grounds that there are numerous scientific and historic mistakes in the text. These seeming disparities in what textual critics have pointed out as apparent flaws in the Scripture have been worked out with other parts of Scripture to show the accuracy of the Bible in history. Besides, over the years, skeptics have pointed to disparities between the Bible and secular accounts only to be proven wrong when archeologists unearth something that proves the Bible's accuracy.

Much more could be said regarding the countless times the world doubted the Bible's accuracy regarding a name or historical personage only to be proved right time after time. For example, the *Tel Dan Inscription* proves the existence of King David, the *Moabite Stone* proves the veracity of the Book of 2 Kings 3, and the

---

[6] For more on the Canon of Scripture, see Michael J. Kruger, *The Question of Canon: Challenging the Status Quo in the New Testament Debate* (Downers Grove, IL: IVP, 2013).

Lachish Letters demonstrate there was a Babylonian captivity.[7] What we find when we allow the Bible to interpret itself is seeming contradictions only seem to be contradictive. What we must do is harmonize these apparent contradictions by other parts of Scripture.

As to the apparent inconsistencies between the findings of science and the facts of the Bible, it must be said that the Bible does not contradict the findings of science, rather the Bible contradicts and opposes the godless Darwinian hypothesis of evolutionary science. The Bible speaks of a creative week, not a drawn-out evolutionary timeline. Further, contrary to the evolutionist theories, the Scripture speaks accurately and decisively about the origin of the universe (Gen 1:1, et al; Mt 19:4-6; Mk 10:5-9; Jn 5:17). As regarding science, let it be said we need not pit science against the Bible, rather we should reject any scientific theory, such as evolution, that denies the biblical account of creation (see chapter five).

As a short answer, let it be said if God didn't create Adam, as the Bible reveals in Genesis, and if we evolved from apes as evolution teaches, then the Adam-Christ parallel that the Apostle Paul reveals is dissolved, and the truth about redemption is destroyed (Rom 5:12-20; 8:23; 1 Cor 15:47-49; Phil 3:21).

Pastors are called to preach and teach the Bible to Christ's sheep. How important is it then for a pastor to have a correct view of Scripture? Having a low view of Scripture is the stumbling block and method of entry for all sorts of biblically condemned practices that are

---

[7] John D. Currid, "10 Crucial Archaeological Discoveries Related to the Bible" available from:
https://www.crossway.org/articles/10-crucial-archaeological-discoveries-related-to-the-bible/ Internet; accessed 17 April 2018.

now celebrated. J.C. Ryle put it best when he wrote, "We corrupt the Word of God most dangerously, when we throw doubt on the plenary inspiration of any part of Holy Scripture."[8] The Bible reveals truth. Truth about God, truth about the world, and truth about ourselves. "Truth," as R.C. Sproul puts it, "is reality as God sees it."

Standing obstinately against this is the spirit of the age. Man redefines terminology in hopes of relieving his troubled conscience. To counter this trend, God's man must define all terms based upon what the Bible claims for itself. Then, objections may be answered according to the Bible's claims. To disregard the Bible's inspiration, sufficiency and authority will lead only to confusion and despair. However, the purer the doctrine, the purer the flow of God's Holy Spirit. Anything short of the belief in the fullness of Scripture as a divine flow of grace is insufficient.

Lastly, the Bible gives life. There is no other book like it. The Bible is sufficient for salvation (Ps 119:97-104; Jn 5:39). All that need be known for life and godliness is clearly revealed in Scripture. The Holy Spirit makes the reading and especially the preaching of the word effectual unto salvation. Moreover, we can never plumb the depths of God's Word. There are depths in it in which the elephant may swim, yet there are shallows where the lamb may wade. As noted by Augustine, "The Bible was composed in such a way that as beginners mature, its meaning grows with them."

This teaches us it is only the ministry of the Word of God that can give life to the dead, restore us, and give

---

[8] J. C. Ryle, *Warning to the Churches* (Carlisle, PA: Banner of Truth, 1967), 25.

us joy and peace with God. There simply is no other Book in the world like the life-giving, soul-restoring Word of God. This is what the Lord Jesus teaches us in Matthew 4:4 when He says: "Man does not live by bread alone, but by every word that proceeds from the mouth of God." How important is it then for a pastor to have a correct view of Scripture?

As pastors, as we guide God's people, we are to do so informed by Scripture. We are to provide Christ's sheep with God's life-giving Word. We are to apply God's Word to every area of our lives. This is what we call theology. Theology is therefore the application of God's word to all areas of life.[9] Pastors equip the saints for the work of ministry and build up the body of Christ with the Word of God (Eph 4:11). In this way, the sheep can live for the glory of God and be protected from error.

---

[9] John Frame, *Doctrine of the Christian Life*, (Philipsburg, NJ: P&R, 2008), 9.

Chapter Four: Doctrine of God

"The grace of the Lord Jesus Christ, and the love of God, and the communion of the Holy Spirit be with you all. Amen." – 2 Corinthians 13:14

Pastors guide God's people to know the God Who has revealed Himself in the Bible. Throughout history there have been many concepts of God. For example, polytheism is the belief in many gods. Henotheism is the belief in a single god among other gods. Pantheism is the belief that the world is divine, and atheism, which claims there is no God. There is one other major world view about God and that is deism. Deism is similar to theism but denies the miraculous, and posits a God who is transcendent over the universe but not immanent within His creation.[1] While God is separate from His creation (transcendent), deism is wrong because God reveals Himself savingly to mankind, and works within His own created order to bring about all things for His glory (immanent).

The knowledge of God is the core doctrine and exclusive content of theology.[2] God is known on the grounds that He has revealed Himself. As revealed in the Holy Scriptures, God has eternally existed as three Persons within the unity of a single divine Being (Mt 28:19; 2 Cor 13:14). See figure 4-1.

---

[1] Norman L. Geisler, *Systematic Theology* (Bloomington, MN: Bethany House, 2002), 18.

[2] Herman Bavinck, *Reformed Dogmatics, Volume 2: God and Man* (Grand Rapids: Baker, 2004), 27.

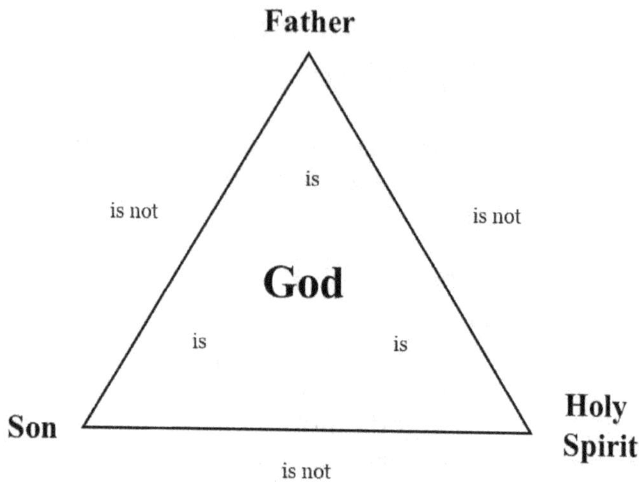

Figure 4-1. The Holy Trinity.

Understanding the diagram above, the Father is God, the Son is God, and the Holy Spirit is God. However, the Father is not the Son, the Son is not the Holy Spirit, and the Holy Spirit is not the Father, etc. God is three Persons, and these three are one God. God is one in essence and three Persons in substance, namely the Father, the Son, and the Holy Spirit; and these three are one God, the same in substance, equal in power and glory. As observed by the Early Church Fathers, as we affirm the doctrine of the Trinity, we espouse the revealed nature of God. "The real mystery of the Trinity," observes Louis Berkhof, "consists in this that each one of the Persons possesses the whole of the divine essence, and that this has no existence outside of and apart from the Persons."[1]

[1] Louis Berkhof, *Summary of Christian Doctrine* (Carlisle, PA: Banner of Truth, 1960), 30.

In the New Testament, the names of God are simply the Greek forms of those found in the Old Testament. For example, the name *Theos*, the most commonly employed name for God in the New Testament, is simply the word used in place of the Hebrew word *Elohim* אֱל הִים. Additionally, the name *Kurios*, used over seven thousand times in the Bible, meaning 'Lord,' is applied not only to God but also to Christ (Phil 2:11; Rev 4:8). This name takes the place of both 'Adonai' and Yahweh.

As the whole Bible teaches, God the Father represents the Trinity. He determined before time began to send His Son to redeem His people and for the Holy Spirit to apply this redemption (Eph 1:3-14). Jesus Christ, the eternal Son, possesses all the divine excellencies, being co-substantial and co-eternal with the Father and the Holy Spirit. In His incarnation, He united to His divine nature a true human nature and so continues to be both God and Man, in two distinct natures and one Person, forever. Jesus is fully God and fully man. His divinity is clearly taught in Scripture (Jn 8:24).

Jesus Christ was conceived by the Holy Spirit, born of the Virgin Mary, fulfilled the requirements of the Law by His sinless life, suffered under Pontius Pilate, poured out His blood as a vicarious and propitiatory atonement for the sins of His people in satisfaction of divine justice. On the third day, Christ was raised from the dead in the same body. He ascended into heaven and is now seated at the right hand of God the Father interceding in Glory for His redeemed (Heb 7:25).

Looking again at 2 Timothy 1:1, Paul says he is an apostle of Jesus Christ by the will of God "according to the promise of life which is in Christ Jesus." God gave Himself in the Person of His Son to suffer instead of us the death, punishment and curse due to fallen humanity as the penalty for sin. This is in fulfillment of Genesis 3:15 which declared that although mankind fell into sin by listening to Satan and rebelling, God, who is gracious and abundant in mercy, would not let the history of mankind end then and there. God's curse for disobedience was death. But the promise of life was that in time, the Seed of the woman would bruise the head of the serpent. The whole Bible is the working out of this prophecy. Jesus is the One through whom God's righteous purpose is finally accomplished – to raise up the ruined posterity of Adam.

The Holy Spirit is Himself God, the Lord and giver of life. He can be lied to (Acts 5:3), and grieved (Eph 4:30). Through the ministry of regeneration and progressive sanctification, the Holy Spirit applies salvation, guides and comforts the children of God, directs and empowers the church in fulfilment of the Great commission, and convicts the world of sin, righteousness, and judgment (Jn 16:7-11).

At the moment of regeneration, the Spirit cultivates Christian character, comforts believers, and bestows spiritual gifts by which they serve God through His church. Looking again at 2 Timothy 1:6, Paul exhorts Timothy to "stir up," literally fan into flame, the gift of God which is in him. The Holy Spirit empowers believers to accomplish the tasks God has prepared for them to do (Eph 2:10).

Moreover, the Holy Spirit seals each believer unto the day of final redemption (Eph 1:14; 1 Tim 4:16). His presence in the Christian is the guarantee that God will bring the believer into the fullness of the stature of

Christ. Thus, salvation is the work of the triune God. Redemption is purposed by the Father, accomplished by the Son, and applied by the Holy Spirit (Ex 3:22; Dt 32:6; Jn 1:1, 8:24). A belief in the Trinity therefore constitutes what the Bible reveals regarding the nature of God. This is therefore a core doctrine of the Church. In fact, as Herman Bavinck relates, "The entire Christian belief system stands or falls with the confession of God's Trinity."[2]

This leads us to consider an important question: What is God's relationship to His creation? As the Bible declares, God is Lord and King. He is the Creator of all things and is separate from His creation. Therefore, we must reject the pantheistic speculations about God. Likewise, God's creation doesn't become divine but remains creation. In light of this, we must understand 2 Peter 1:4 which declares that through the promises we may "partake of the divine nature," to refer not to essence but rather to a moral and ethical sense. In other words, God develops the image of Jesus in us by faith. God is therefore separate from His creation but transcends it in order to reveal Himself savingly to mankind.

God also reveals Himself in the Bible by His divine names. For instance, God reveals Himself as El-Shaddai, which means 'God Almighty,' to Abraham, Isaac and Jacob (Ex 6:2-3); a name which not only signifies God's greatness, but a source of comfort and blessing as well. The greatest name of God is Yahweh (Jehovah). The name's origin and meaning are indicated in Exodus chapter three. Moses said to God:

---

[2] Bavinck, *Reformed Dogmatics*, 333.

> "Indeed, when I come to the children of Israel and say to them, 'The God of your fathers has sent me to you,' and they say to me, 'What is His name?' what shall I say to them?" 14 And God said to Moses, "I AM WHO I AM." And He said, "Thus you shall say to the children of Israel, 'I AM has sent me to you.'"" (Ex 3:13-14).

When God says, "I AM WHO I AM," this expresses the fact that God is always the same, is self-existent, and especially, it means He is "unchangeable in His covenant relationship and is always faithful to His promises."[3]

God also reveals Himself by way of His attributes. For instance, God is a Spirit, infinite, eternal, and unchangeable, in His being (self-existent), wisdom, power, holiness, justice, goodness, and truth.[4] Moreover, God is love personified (1 Jn 4:8). God has eternally existed as Father, Son, and Holy Spirit, with distinct personal attributes, but without division of nature, essence, or being (1 Jn 5:7; Mt 28:19; 2 Cor 13:14).

Our relationship with the personal God of the Bible is based on God's written revelation and the finished work of Jesus Christ. As pastors, we are to guide God's people to know the God Who has revealed Himself in the Bible. As we preach and teach God's Word to His people, in increasing ways, they will come to know the triune God.

---

[3] Louis Berkhof, *Summary of Christian Doctrine* (Carlisle, PA: Banner of Truth, 1960), 32.
[4] Westminster Shorter Catechism Answer 4.

Chapter Five: Doctrine of Man

"For it pleased God, after He had made all things by the word of His power, to create man after His own image." – George Whitefield

The Christian Faith presupposes a belief that humanity is fallen in Adam's original sin, and as such is dead, defiled and under God's condemning wrath (Jn 3:36). In other words, according to Christianity, humanity has no future without Jesus. With this presupposed, the aim of this chapter is to consider four things: (1) Creation of man, (2) cultural mandate, (3) covenant of works, and (4) covenant of marriage.

Creation of Man

God spoke into existence everything out of nothing. Before the universe was made, it existed only in the mind of God. The Book of Genesis tells us that God created the universe and everything in it in six twenty-four-hour periods. On the sixth day, God created man. As the special creation of God, man is made in God's own image (Gen 1:26). God created mankind male and female as the crowning work of His creation. This raises something very important. Many believe that science has disproved the Bible and Christianity. They find the Bible to be incompatible with the theory of evolution, which envisions an endless string of revolutionary mutations between primordial soup and modern man. Many Christians, try to accommodate the theory of evolution by proposing that the creation account of Genesis should be understood symbolically and they espouse a view known as theistic evolution. However, the major problem with evolution is that it envisions mankind as just a random mutation over billions of years. In this vein, Richard Dawkins famously observes:

> In a universe of electrons and selfish genes, blind physical forces and genetic replication, some people are going to get hurt, other people are going to get lucky, and you won't find any rhyme or reason in it, nor any justice. The universe that we observe has precisely the properties we should expect if there is, at bottom, no design, no purpose, no evil, no good, nothing but pitiless indifference.[1]

According to those like Dawkins, what is our purpose here on earth? There is none, only random chance.

Evolution is a lie because it involves endless mutations and death. In other words, evolution envisions death before the fall. Further, let it be said that theistic evolution is science-driven rather than Scripture driven. Over against evolution, let it be said that order is heaven's first law. Ironically, in their efforts to appear scientifically savvy, Christians who pander to such scientific speculations genuflect toward Darwin, undermine the authority of the Scripture, lose credibility, and disrespect Jesus Christ.

The Bible tells us that God formed Adam, which in Hebrew means "man," out of the dust of the earth, "and

---

[1] Richard Dawkins, *River Out of Eden: A Darwinian View of Life* (New York, NY: Basic Books, 1995), 133.

breathed into his nostrils the breath of life: and man became a living being" (Gen 2:7).[2] The Bible also presents Adam as the first man and Jesus Christ as the second Man: "The first man was of the earth, made of dust; the second Man is the Lord from heaven (1 Cor 15:47)." Touching on the truth of redemption, if evolution was true, then the Adam-Christ parallel of the New Testament is meaningless (Rom 5:12).

Further, our preaching would be empty. Christ took upon Himself our likeness and our infirmities yet without sin. In the final analysis, if God didn't create Adam and we evolved from apes, or any previous types of life forms which had decomposed, or whatever, then the Adam-Christ parallel is dissolved, and Christ is not in fact the second Man, and the truth about redemption is destroyed (Rom 5:12-20; 8:23; 1 Cor 15:47-49; Phil 3:21). The unassumed is unredeemed. The theory of evolution, which states that mankind is evolved from apes, is therefore incompatible with the Word of God, and should be rejected by Christians.

There is another theory called the "gap theory" which has plagued the church. This theory posits a gap of thousands or even millions of years between Genesis 1:1 and 1:2. This view envisions God making mankind before the creation account of Gen 1:26, and that a supposed satanic rebellion ruined the earth at that time. However, this view must also be rejected because its unbiblical. The Bible never states that God created

---

[2] As we consider Genesis 2, it is often asked: Why two creation accounts? Let it be said, what we have is not evidence of an editor patching together different sources but is the normal pattern of Hebrew narrative to consider a topic in a resumptive manner. And so, while the first creation story in 1:1–2:3 gives a global perspective. The second creation story in 2:4–3:24 focuses on the creation of man. Thus, the first focuses on the origin of the universe and the second on humanity.

man before Adam. Rather in Genesis 1:26, the creation of man is spoken of as having been planned within the council of the Godhead, with the express purpose of being able to take part in life of God.

The Bible teaches us that God created man and placed him in paradise. Man was created flesh out of God's created dust. God actualized this flesh by His creative breath, creating man's invisible component, his soul. Man's soul is a direct creation of God and is not pre-existent (Gen 2:7). Man is God's special creation; we bear God's image. Mankind resembles God in some way. But in which way?

One way is mankind bears certain of God's attributes, namely His rationality, His personality and morality. In other words, we image or reflect God in these ways. Another way we are made in the image of God is we have certain unique qualities which are unparalleled in the rest of God's creation. For example, we are endowed with a spirit which goes on forever. Because of this unique spiritual and immortal aspect to man's existence, man was originally designed by God to go on forever, and enjoy fellowship with God. With this understanding, it may be said: God created man in His own image and designed him with the express purpose of being able to enjoy fellowship with Him and take part in His life. Additionally, because we bear the image of God, man's life is sacred. This is why capital crimes, such as murder, are to be punished by the taking of life, because of the image of God in man.

God's image in us also points to the fact that we were created to rule the earth as God's representative. This is why in Genesis 1:26 God says:

> "Let them have dominion (that is lordship and authority) over the fish of the sea, over the birds of the air, and over the cattle, over all the earth and over every creeping thing that creeps on the earth."

Mankind is the crowning work of God's creation. God created man to be His representative ruler on the earth, to have dominion over the rest of His creation.

So, when we say that man was created in the image of God, we intend this to mean that man inhabits the invisible realm by virtue of his soul, and the physical realm by virtue of his body. Being created in the image of God may also refer to man's being endued with a mind, will and emotions. Additionally, the Bible teaches us that God created man in a state of original righteousness and made man spiritually, physically, and morally perfect (Gen 1:31).

Cultural Mandate

When God created man, He also established certain blessings and obligations for him which has often called the 'cultural mandate.' In Genesis 1:27-28 we are told:

> '"So God created man in His own image; in the image of God He created him; male and female He created them. Then God blessed them, and God said to them, "Be fruitful and multiply."'

This cultural mandate is also referred to as the mandate of procreation. Notice first, God created only two genders: male and female. God's command is be fruitful and multiply. What should be understood is this procreation mandate is in connection with the marriage ordinance. In other words, this command of God was to be expressed only within the bonds of a mutual commitment called marriage. With this understanding, the divine command is:

> "Fill the earth and subdue it; have dominion over the fish of the sea, over the birds of the air, and over every living thing that moves on the earth" (Gen 1:28).

I wonder if you have ever considered the connection between God's cultural mandate (Gen 1:28) and His Great commission (Mt 28:18-20)? As you recall, God's purpose in creating man was to have him reflect His glory, to be an image bearer. And that essentially is what the cultural mandate is all about, making more image bearers of God, making more worshippers of God. God's intent in given us the cultural mandate was that as His image bearers we would fill the earth, then the whole earth would be filled with the glory of God as waters cover the sea (Hab 2:14: Eph 1:22-23). And my friends, that also is what the cultural mandate and Great Commission is all about.

Mankind was created in the image of God to have fellowship with God and reflect (image) Him, and be fruitful and multiply, creating others who would likewise reflect the glory of God. Why are we here? God created man in His own image and purposed for him to fill the earth with more worshippers.

What is noteworthy is the fact that God blessed mankind from the very beginning. God could have treated man as He treated the other animals if He had wanted to. Man had done nothing to earn this particular favor that God was showing him. God also graciously provides food for man for all the animals of the earth (Gen 1:30).

Covenant of Works

In this original relationship between God and Adam prior to the fall, God gave both vast privileges and certain obligations. In the garden of Eden, the Lord sets down both blessings and obligations. Genesis 2:8-9, 15-17 tells us:

> The Lord God planted a garden eastward in Eden, and there He put the man whom He had formed. And out of the ground the Lord God made every tree grow that is pleasant to the sight and good for food. The tree of life was also in the midst of the garden, and the tree of the knowledge of good and evil...Then the Lord God took the man and put him in the garden of Eden to tend and keep it. And the Lord God commanded the man, saying, "Of every tree of the garden you may freely eat; but of the tree of the knowledge of good and evil you shall not eat, for in the day that you eat of it you shall surely die."

God provided food for man and placed two trees in the garden among all the other trees: the tree of life, and the tree of the knowledge of good and evil. If Adam is faithful, there is the prospect of the tree of life and eternal fellowship with God. If he is unfaithful, he shall surely die.

As the Bible demonstrates, a covenant is a special relationship established and bestowed by God that has both blessings and obligations. O. Palmer Robertson described the covenant as "A bond in blood sovereignly administered."[3] This is a shorthand way of describing humanity's relationship to God. It's a life and death relationship (bond in blood) with attendant blessings and obligations, bestowed and administered by God Himself (sovereignly administered).

In light of the cultural mandate we have discussed, as "God took the man and put him in the garden of Eden to tend and keep it," we are reminded that labor was originally good (Gen 2:15). God placed Adam in the garden to work. This reminds us of the cultural mandate God established for man in the very beginning. It was God's purpose for man to labor so that he would have dominion over the earth. God therefore placed Adam in the garden to labor, to take dominion over it, and bring it to fullness. This also reminds us of the fact that work is not inherently bad.

Additionally, as God's image bearer, Adam was also to follow the Lord's example by resting from his work. God did not need to rest as if He were physically exhausted, but His pattern of work and rest in six days and then a seventh of rest was designed specifically for us because He knew that we needed that rest from our labor (Gen 2:2).

Then there are obligations. There is a specific prohibition, "Of every tree of the garden you may freely eat; but of the tree of the knowledge of good and evil you shall not eat." And there's a consequence and penalty attached to that. The Lord says, "In the day that you eat of it, you shall surely die." In this we see a special relationship between God and Adam, which has

---

[3] O. Palmer Robertson, *The Christ of the Covenants* (Phillipsburg, NJ: P&R, 1980), 4.

both privileges and obligations, as well as life and death consequences.

The tree of life was a sacrament, a sign of a promise that God has implied. The other tree is a test. The covenant of works therefore was a relationship that was conditioned upon Adam's obedience. God's covenant stipulations sanctioned death for disobedience and life for obedience. The reality of the covenant of works is everyone born in Adam are dead, defiled, and damned; and will remain so unless Christ's redemption is applied to them (Mt 11:27). This is because God made a covenant of works with Adam and his posterity whereby Adam, and all of us, were promised life for obedience and death for disobedience.

As it will be shown later, covenant is our relationship with God, either the covenant of works or the covenant of grace. Under the covenant of grace, Jesus Christ accomplished what Adam failed to do in the covenant of works. The essence of the covenant of grace is the same throughout the Old and New Testaments – God saves sinners by grace alone, through faith alone, in Christ alone. No one has ever been saved by works of the law, only grace (Gal 2:16; 3:11).

Covenant of Marriage

The culminating blessing that God granted to Adam in the garden was God's creation of woman. Knowing man's need for intimacy and for companionship with a peer, God created woman. Having created the woman from the man, God created the covenant of marriage which is the crowning blessing of God's goodness to humanity. God in His good providence recognized the social needs of man for companionship even in paradise:

> 18 And the Lord God said, "It is not good that man should be alone; I will make him a helper comparable to him." 19 Out of the ground the Lord God formed every beast of the field and every bird of the air, and brought them to Adam to see what he would call them. And whatever Adam called each living creature, that was its name. 20 So Adam gave names to all cattle, to the birds of the air, and to every beast of the field. But for Adam there was not found a helper comparable to him (Gen 2:18-20).

In verses 18-20, we learn that God simultaneously made Adam aware of his need for a companion and allowed him to express his dominion in the naming of the animals (cf. Gen 1:26). Adam's naming of the animals demonstrates that he has headship, authority and dominion.

"But for Adam there was not found a helper comparable to him," that is a suitable counterpart. The Hebrew word for comparable, נֶגֶד *neged* also means opposite. In fact, the phrase "a helper comparable" indicates a perfect fit. What this passage also shows is God Himself makes provision for Adam's need, creating for him a "helper comparable to him." Genesis 2:21-25 declares:

> 21 And the Lord God caused a deep sleep to fall on Adam, and he slept; and He took one of his ribs, and closed up the flesh in its place. 22 Then the rib which the Lord God had taken from man He made into a woman, and He brought her to the man. 23 And Adam said: "This is now bone of my bones and flesh of my flesh; she shall be called Woman, because she

> was taken out of Man." 24 Therefore a man shall leave his father and mother and be joined to his wife, and they shall become one flesh. 25 And they were both naked, the man and his wife, and were not ashamed.

Notice first of all, man is first formed from the ground, and then woman is formed from him. The Apostle Paul stresses that this is very significant for the relationships between man and woman, especially between a husband and wife (1 Tim 2:13). Additionally, Paul relates back to this in 1 Corinthians 11:8-9 and notes that woman was made for man, that is to be a suitable helper to him. Not only that but in 1 Corinthians 11:7, Paul states that Eve is the crown and glory of Adam.

Also significant is the fact that Adam sleeps while woman is made so he can never take credit for her creation. God brings woman into existence and Adam names her "woman" showing again the authority God has given to him. This also shows compatibility, Adam says: "This is now bone of my bones and flesh of my flesh; she shall be called Woman, because she was taken out of Man" (Gen 2:23). In Hebrew man is *ish*, woman is *isha*. Tellingly, woman is derived from man as her name is derived from his. The whole account demonstrates God's created order as well as woman's equality and compatibility with man.

The fact that man slept while God created woman points to a wonderful truth about Christ and the church. Adam's sleep is likened to the death of Christ and the creation of the Church. In this vein, Horatius Bonar observed: "There must be sleep in the first Adam before God can take out of him the ordained spouse.

And there must be death in the second Adam before God can take out of Him the chosen bride."[4]

Likewise, Matthew Henry observed: "The woman was made of a rib out of the side of Adam, not made out of his head to rule over him, nor out of his feet to be trampled upon by him, but out of his side to be equal with him; under his arm to be protected and near his heart to be beloved." Woman is the culminating blessing God granted to Adam. Like a father of the bride, God leads the woman to the man (Gen 2:22).

Additionally, as Derek Kidner notes: "The woman is presented wholly as man's partner and counterpart. Nothing yet is said of her child bearing. She is valued for herself alone."[5] That being said, fertility does not make a woman valuable to her husband in and of itself. She is valuable to her husband regardless of whatever procreative blessings the Lord showers on that family.

Marriage is therefore the God-ordained institution on which the family, as well as society as a whole is founded. As it is the most ancient of all societies and the only natural one. God created marriage for the mutual help of husband and wife, to provide mankind with a legitimate issue, and to give the Church a holy progeny. Marriage is the bedrock on which the family is built, nourished and protected. As Jesus Christ taught, marriage is the uniting of one man and one woman in a covenant commitment for a lifetime (Mt 19:4-6).

Therefore, rather than being merely a contract for a limited amount of time, conditioned upon the performance of contractual obligations by the other

---

[4] Horatius Bonar, *Earth's Morning or Thoughts on Genesis* (New York, NY: Robert Carter, 1875), 87.
[5] Derek Kidner, *Genesis* (Downers Grove, IL: IVP, 1967), 70.

partner, marriage is a life-long sacred bond that is characterized by permanence, sacredness, intimacy, mutuality, and exclusiveness. Verse 25 states: "And they were both naked, the man and his wife, and were not ashamed." Sexual intimacy, a gift of God to be enjoyed between a man and woman within the marriage covenant, is forbidden outside of marriage. It's significant when we realize that creation wasn't complete until God created the family.

The Fall of Man

As the Bible teaches, God not only made man, He also made creatures called angels, who are spiritual beings endowed with great power. One of these angels rebelled against God and persuaded others to follow him (Rev 12:7-9). But God smote him and he fell. "The Bible tells us that this terrible, dread spiritual power, called Satan and the Devil, entered into this world, into God's perfect creation, and by tempting the man and woman whom God had made brought about to pass everything bad that you and I know."[6]

Genesis two finds Adam enjoying perfect fellowship with God and his wife. He was to tend the Garden with the goal of filling the earth with more image-bearers, subduing it, so that the whole earth would be like Eden, a garden paradise sanctuary at perfect peace with God. There were also certain things Adam and Eve were to refrain from doing. In particular, the eating of the tree of the knowledge of good and evil. Under this "covenant of works," the prospects of the tree of life,

---

[6] David M. Lloyd-Jones, *The Gospel in Genesis: From Fig Leaves to Faith* (Wheaton, IL: Crossway, 2009), 18.

which pointed to eternal life, for perfect obedience was held out, as well as death for disobedience. As Genesis two closes, Adam and Eve are living in perfect bliss with God and with each other, having been brought together to live in the God-ordained institution of marriage. And that's where Satan took aim.

In a recent survey conducted by the Barna Group, some 1800 self-ascribed Christians were asked if they believed the devil was real. Fifty percent of those polled said the devil didn't really exist, and ten percent said they weren't sure. But that's it, isn't it? As Keyser Söze once put it: "The greatest trick the Devil ever pulled was convincing the world that he didn't exist." But the Bible is the only Book that tells us how evil came into the world.

The Tempter doesn't start off immediately by contradicting God, rather he asks a question that is designed to plant a seed of doubt. He asks "Has God indeed said, 'You shall not eat of every tree of the garden'?" And Eve says: "God has said, 'You shall not eat it, nor shall you touch it, lest you die.'" Yet when God gave the command in Gen 2, there was no mention of a prohibition against touching the fruit, only eating it. In this way, Eve makes the mistake of adding to God's Word, and by doing so, she makes God's command more strict than it was. As God's men, we are to take care neither to add to nor take away from God's words (Dt 12:32; Rev 22:18-19).

Satan's aim was to get Eve to question God's wisdom and judgment. And the very first doctrine that was ever denied was the doctrine of judgment. Satan lies: "You will not surely die" (Gen 3:4). In light of the disparaging statistics mentioned earlier, don't think that the modern denial of God's judgment and hell is anything new. These were the very first doctrines ever denied. Satan has been a liar from the beginning, and here's the big lie: "You will not surely die."

Adding to this lie, Satan sought to malign the character of God and said: "For God knows that in the day you eat of it your eyes will be opened, and you will be like God, knowing good and evil." Here's the demonic lie: God is trying to keep you down. He's not really for you. He doesn't really want you to take part in His life. If you eat the forbidden fruit, you'll be as wise and as powerful as Him. In other words, Satan is saying, by refusing you access to that tree; God is only pretending to care for you. He is a hard Master. And Satan's tactics haven't changed a bit. He still seeks to malign God's character, and presents God as our enemy. What was really being offered by Satan I think was this: "You can set yourself up on your own. You don't need God or His rules."

Then, in Gen 3:6 are the devil's three modes of temptation: (1) Eve saw that the tree was good for food, this, as 1 John 2 tells us is the lust of the flesh, it's the desire to gratify the body. (2) Then, she saw that it was pleasant to the eyes, this is the lust of the eyes, which is covetousness. And third (3), she saw that the tree was desirable to make one wise, this is, the pride of life, a sinful desire for status or knowledge.

Interestingly, Satan says to the two human beings most like God, if you'll sin, you'll be like God. He was offering them something that they already had, they were already made in God's image. But in following his suggestions, they lost their original righteousness and communion with God. They took the devil's bait, hook, line and sinker. Using a fishing illustration, Mark Driscoll observes:

> The key to catching fish is knowing what kind of bait they like. Once you get the right bait on the hook, the rest is pretty easy. You drop it in front of the fish, they swim up, bite the bait, and overlook the hook. You would think that at some point the fish would catch on to this ploy. Nope. The fish never learn, and the same old bait-and-hook method works every time. And people are a lot like fish. The devil and his demons figure out what kind of bait we like and dangle it in front of us. Like a fisherman, the devil couldn't care less what bait we prefer. He will gladly give us sex, money, power, success, comfort, drugs, alcohol—pick a preference. And like fish, we continually swim right on up and take the bait and forget about the hook.[7]

If you follow the analogy of the baited-hook, temptation is not sin in itself, its giving into temptation that leads to sin (Jam 1:12-15). When we're tempted, there's a moment when we are offered some type of forbidden fruit and we have to choose between God's commands and the gratification of sin.

When we're tempted, we are to follow the example of our Savior Jesus Christ. As Matthew 4 tells us, when Jesus was tempted by the devil in the wilderness, the Lord resisted him and rebuked him at every turn with Scripture. To help us when we're tempted, we can remember five "R"s:

1. Recognize. When you are being tempted, recognize it for what it is.

---

[7] Mark Driscoll, "Your Weapons to Defeat the Devil," available from: https://www.bible.com/reading-plans/12568-spirit-filled-jesus-weapons-to-defeat-the-devil/day/4; Internet; accessed 17 April 2018.

2. Resist. James 4:7 tells us to "resist the devil and he will flee from you." 2 Timothy 2:22 tells us to "flee youthful lusts." This may involve running out of a room like Joseph. Or fleeing mentally as Paul says in 2 Cor 10:5 when he says: "Hold all thoughts captive to the Lord."

3. Rebuke. Rebuke the enemy in Jesus' name (Zech 3:2; Jude 9).

4. Repent. Maybe it's got to the point where you've entertained sinful thoughts and already begin to sin in your mind.

5. Request God's strength. The Lord says in Ps 50:15, "Call upon Me in the day of your trouble and I will deliver you and you shall glory Me." But our first parents did not resist the temptation.

Taking the devil's bait, Eve "took of its fruit and ate. She also gave to her husband with her, and he ate." And so, we see sin is the result of following the suggestions of Satan. After they sinned, their "eyes were opened," they saw they had been deceived by the serpent. They saw their privileges vanish: communion with God, dominion over the creatures, and the purity and holiness of their nature, gone in one instantaneous ruinous defection from God's command. Then, sin leads to shame. And so, they sewed fig leaves together to cover themselves.

Another consequence of sin is blame shifting: When God questions Adam, what does he say? "The woman whom You gave to be with me, she gave me of the tree, and I ate." In other words, it's ultimately Your fault and her fault. I didn't do anything! But Adam was no innocent bystander. He defected from God's command. He failed to protect his wife from the serpent. He failed to take responsibility by not assuming his God-given role as the spiritual leader of the family. He should've hacked that snake to pieces. Men may want to blame others for everything that's wrong in the world but the reality is it's our fault. Then in verse 13, the Lord God said to the woman: "What is this you have done?"

The woman said, "The serpent deceived me, and I ate." Notice, sin brings shame, disrupts fellowship and makes cowards of us all: Eve says, the devil made me do it, and Adam blames everyone but himself.

By contrast, we are reminded that Jesus offered no retort or defense when He was falsely accused. And in silence, He bore the guilt and the sin that belonged to us so that we could be credited, not with blame, but with His perfect righteousness.

God then brings judgment on all of the parties involved in this rebellion. God begins by judging Satan by way of the serpent, with the harshest condemnation of all, and in the curse, He announces the first gospel – the *protoevangelium*. God says: "And I will put enmity between you and the woman, and between your seed and her Seed; He shall bruise your head, and you shall bruise His heel" (Gen 3:15).

God says, there will come from the woman One who will destroy everything that you are. Jesus is the Seed of the woman, and the whole Bible is a playing out of this prophecy. Moreover, this passage is absolutely essential to the understanding of the gospel because without an understanding of sin and of our culpability, we cannot understand grace and we cannot embrace grace.[8] Right there, God's promise is given. God pronounces that the redemption that will be accomplished will involve the perpetual conflict of the Woman's Seed and the seed of the serpent. God curses the serpent and judges man but even in judgment, God blesses man.

Genesis 3:15 is therefore a one-verse summary of God's promise of redemption. It traces the outlines of the doctrine of the Incarnation and of the Virgin Birth; it prophesies the crucifixion; and of the final overthrow of Satan. By this promise, God gives mankind hope in regards to their struggle against Satan. And to keep them from being completely overpowered by him, God graciously places an enmity, that is, a deep-seated hostility between the Seed of the Woman and the seed of the serpent. And through this hostility, God declares He will reassert His rule over the earth in accordance with His plan.

This promise is that one day the Seed of the Woman would come, and in close combat with the serpent, though He would be mortally wounded, He would crush the head of the serpent. The word for bruise in the Hebrew is שׁוּף *shoof*, which in addition to bruise means to break or grind. What we have in Genesis 3:14-19 is salvation through judgment. Ironically, as noted by Ligon Duncan:

> The curses of Genesis 3 are the first step forward in the covenant of grace. in these words of curse, blessing is implied and combined. also, the creational ordinances of marriage and labor, and even by a very subtle implication the Sabbath, remain in force as continuing responsibilities as is

---

[8] Ibid.

> seen in the very curses that the Lord administers in His sentence against the serpent and the woman and finally Adam. And, as he notes, there is also a movement towards restoration even in these words of penalty.[9]

Mankind, though created in the image of God, has fallen in Adam but as the prophecy of Gen 3:15 points forward, those of faith in Christ are raised to life, and have restored fellowship with God (Rom 5:12-21). See figure 3-1.

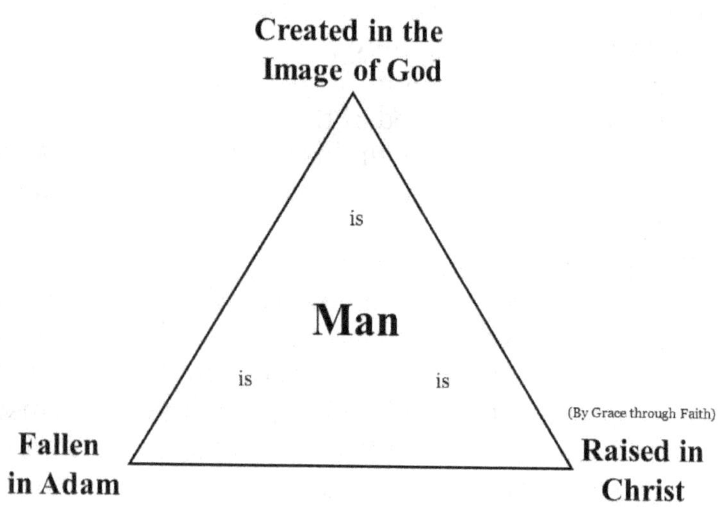

Figure 3-1. Mankind.

Then God turns to the woman and says here is your judgment: "I will greatly multiply your sorrow and your conception; in pain you shall bring forth children; your desire shall be for your husband, and he shall rule over you" (Gen 3:16). With this pronouncement Eve and her

[9] Ligon Duncan, *The Blessings of the Curses: The Serpent.*

daughters would experience increased pain bearing children.

There evidently would have been some pain in the process of bearing children before the Fall, but now womankind would experience increased pain. And women will *desire to control* their men (Gen 3:16). We know this is the proper meaning of this verse because of Gen 4:6-7 which says, "So the Lord said to Cain, "Why are you angry? And why has your countenance fallen? If you do well, will you not be accepted? And if you do not do well, sin lies at the door. And its *desire* is for you, but you should rule over it." Sin desires to master Cain, and Eve desires to master or dominate Adam.

"Your desire shall be for your husband, and he shall *rule* over you" (Gen 3:16). This is not a loving rule, for without Christ it is a domineering, harsh rule. Without the power of Christ, a husband will only selfishly seek to dominate his wife instead of sacrificially loving her. Headship and submission are not introduced in Genesis chapter three but are introduced back in chapter two. The wife was created for the husband. Eve was created by God to be Adam's helper. God completed Adam by creating a wife out of him to be his companion. This is also what 1 Cor 11:3 tells us: "But I want you to know that the head of every man is Christ, the head of woman is man, and the head of Christ is God." Also 1 Cor 11:8 tells us "For man is not from woman, but woman from man. Nor was man created for the woman, but woman for the man." It was only after the Fall that the husband no longer leads easily; he must contend for his headship.

Sin has corrupted both the willing submission of the wife and the loving headship of the husband. The woman's desire without Christ is to control her husband, her divinely appointed leader in the marriage. And so "the rule of love founded in paradise is replaced by struggle, tyranny, domination, and manipulation."[10]

Then God turns to the man and says in effect, as the result of your disobedience, creation will suffer a curse and began to deteriorate. In Genesis chapter two Adam received the privilege of enjoying the garden, but this did not require strenuous labor. Now God tells Adam that he will have to toil hard to obtain a living from the ground. And that he will die rather than live forever experiencing physical immortality.

God says that because of the fall, mankind's natural inclination will be to worry excessively over where their next meal would come from. Without Christ, this will always be the plight of man. Gerhard von Rad observes, "The woman's punishment struck at the deepest root of her being as wife and mother. The man's strikes at the innermost nerve of his life; his work, his activity, and provision for sustenance."[11] And Allen Ross shows, "These punishments represent retaliatory justice. Adam and Eve sinned by eating; they would suffer in order to eat. She manipulated her husband; she would be mastered by her husband."[12]

Adam, having indulged his lust, not being content with his present condition, despised God's command, became enslaved to the Devil, was justly condemned to die (Rom 5:12-21), and thrust out of paradise (Gen 3:20-24). When Adam sinned, God passed the sentence of death on him and his posterity, that is, all

---

[10] Westminster Theological Journal 37:3 (Spring 1975), 376-383.
[11] Gerhard von Rad, *Genesis*, 94.
[12] Ross, *Genesis*, 33.

of us (Rom 5:12). This is the doctrine the church calls original sin.

Adam, representing all mankind, has by his disobedience, brought the curse of death and condemnation on us all. Adam's sin and guilt have been imputed to all mankind, who remain under the curse of death and condemnation unless God in His grace saves them (Jn 3:36). This doctrine of the church, called original sin, is very unpopular. In fact, it has never been popular, because who wants to say we're sinners? This is what led Bertrand Russell to write, "When you hear people in church, debasing themselves and saying that they are miserable sinners, and all the rest of it, it seems contemptible and not worthy of self-respecting human beings."[13] But that is precisely what God demands (Jer 3:13; Acts 2:21; Rom 10:9-10, 13).

Let it also be said, though its popular these days to describe death as merely a natural part of life, a so-called beautiful circle of life, death is judgment. It's neither natural nor beautiful, it's ugly and unnatural. How sad it all is, and to think, this is all many have to look forward to: a life of sickness and pain and then eternal death. And without Christ, this will always be the plight of man. No hope and no future.

After the sentence of death, Adam heard God's promise of redemption, and by faith he "called his wife's name Eve because she was the mother of all living" (Gen 3:20). Adam believed God's promise that one day, the Seed of the Woman would destroy the one who destroyed them, and would reverse the effects of the Fall, and regain Paradise, and their righteousness.

---

[13] Russell, Why I am not a Christian: and Other Essays on Religion and Related Subjects, 23.

Something else that points us to Christ and His redeeming work is the actions of God in Gen 3:21. Fallen man, now needs to be clothed: "Also for Adam and his wife the Lord God made tunics of skin, and clothed them." The Lord provides Adam and Eve more suitable clothing than they had come up with for themselves. What God does is He takes an animal and slays it, and provides its hide to be used as clothing for Adam and Eve.

By this we see another foreshadowing of the gospel: An innocent animal is taken and is put to death not because it had done anything wrong, but because Adam and Eve had done something wrong. It died the death they deserved to die. And this of course, is a picture of what Jesus Christ did for us on our behalf. Jesus is our innocent substitute. He died in our place the death we deserved, and His righteousness is accounted to us by faith so that we are clothed in His righteousness.

One final thing in Genesis three, God removes Adam and Eve from their nearness to the tree of life. God drove Adam and his wife out of the garden and placed cherubim at the east of the garden of Eden, and a flaming sword to guard the way to the tree of life (Gen 3:22-24). Here's another judgment in which man finds grace. God sent them out of the garden lest by eating of the tree in an unworthy manner, they would confirm themselves in a permanent state of condemnation. In other words, they would live forever disfellowshipped. Moreover, the cherubim and flaming sword at the entrance to the garden indicates the absolute impossibility of a human initiated re-establishment of relations with God.

This chapter has been an effort to show that man on his own initiative cannot re-enter into paradise. The only way back is through Christ. Christ's work does more than just reverse the effects of sin, it transforms us, and clothes us in His righteousness, so that we bear His image. And as image-bearers, we are called to fill the earth with image-bearers (Gen 1:26; Mt 28:18-20).

As this chapter also demonstrates, humanity is distinct from the animal creation and not just a higher animal or the most evolved or developed animal. Having been made in the image of God, humanity is God's special creation and has certain unique qualities which are unparalleled in the rest of God's creation such as God's rationality, His personality, His morality. Additionally, mankind is endowed with a spirit which lives on forever. In these ways, mankind reflects God.

Further, it is also evident from Scripture that mankind was created to enjoy fellowship with God and take part in His life. It is for these reasons that man's life is sacred and therefore abortion, racism, human trafficking and exploitation is condemned by Scripture and are not to be tolerated. Moreover, this is why murder is to be punished by the taking of life, because of the image of God in man. Though abortion is widely practiced in our society, it is a legalized form of murder. Abortion is the unauthorized taking of a preborn human life, which is contrary to God's will.

As Christ's undershepherds, it will be healthy and beneficial for the sheep to be taught their real condition which is fallen in Adam but raised to walk in newness of life in Christ (Rom 6:1-11; Col 3:1-7).

Chapter Six: Doctrine of Christ and the Holy Spirit

"The doctrine of redemption is the distinguishing doctrine of the Bible. The person and work of the Redeemer is therefore the great theme of the sacred writers." – Charles Hodge

In light of what we have surveyed in the previous chapter, the promise of God in Genesis 3:15 is the guarantee of redemption that would be accomplished by the Son of God (the Seed of the Woman) and applied by the Holy Spirit. This chapter will therefore discuss the Persons and work of both the Son of God and the Holy Spirit.

According to the Bible, everyone belongs to one of either two covenants – that of Adam and the covenant of works (Gen 1:27; Rom 5:12), or of Christ, the second Adam, and the covenant of grace (Gen 15: Ps 50:5; Rom 5:15-21). Due to the nature of the work that He was to accomplish (Gen 3:15), it was therefore necessary that Jesus Christ should be both God and man. It has been well said that the unassumed is unredeemed. It was therefore necessary that the Son of God should assume the nature of those He came to save (Heb 2:14).

Therefore, what the Church has believed and taught for twenty centuries is: Jesus Christ is the Seed of the woman born to crush the head of the serpent (Gen 3:15). As the eternal Son of God, Jesus Christ possesses all the divine excellencies of God, being co-substantial and co-eternal with the Father and with the Holy Spirit. In His incarnation, the Son of God united to His divine nature a true human nature, and so continues to be both God and Man, in two distinct natures and one

Person, forever. As the Bible teaches, Jesus Christ, the God-Man was conceived by the Holy Spirit, born of the Virgin Mary, fulfilled the requirements of the Law by His sinless life, suffered under Pontius Pilate, poured out His blood as a vicarious and propitiatory atonement for the sins of His people in satisfaction of divine justice, and on the third day was raised from the dead in the same body, now glorified. He ascended into heaven and is now seated at the right hand of God the Father interceding in Glory for His redeemed (Heb 7:25).

For the redemption of God's elect, the Bible reveals that Jesus Christ fulfills a threefold role of Prophet, Priest and King (See figure 6-1).

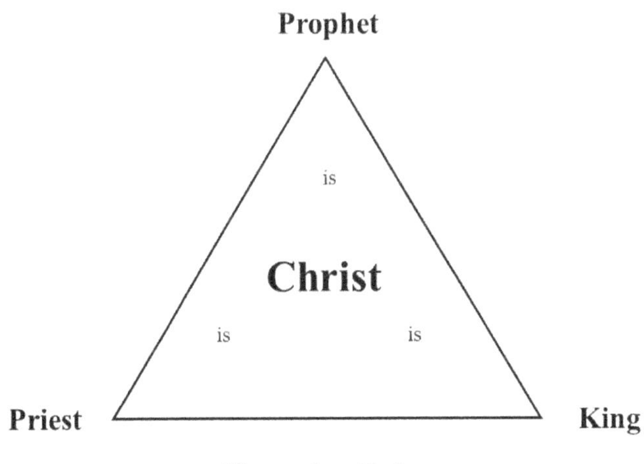

Figure 6-1. Christ.

Christ, the Prophet – It pleased God, in His eternal purpose, to choose and ordain the Lord Jesus, His only begotten Son, to be the Mediator between God and man, the Prophet, Priest, and King, the Head and Savior of His Church, the Heir of all things, and Judge of the world: unto whom He did from all eternity give a people, to be His seed, and to be by Him in time redeemed, called, justified, sanctified, and glorified (Rom 8:29-30). Christ executes the office of a prophet, in His revealing to the church, in all ages, by His Spirit and word, in different ways of administration, the whole will of God, in all things concerning their edification and salvation (Dt 18:15).

Christ, the High Priest – Christ executes the office of a priest, in His once offering Himself a sacrifice without spot to God, to be a reconciliation for the sins of His people; and in making continual intercession for them. The covenant of grace was made with Christ the second Adam, and in Him with all the elect as His seed (Gal 3:16). The grace of God is manifested in the second covenant, in that He freely provided and offered to sinners a mediator, and life and salvation by him; and requiring faith as the condition to interest them in him, promises and gives his Holy Spirit to all His elect, to work in them that faith, with all other saving graces; and to enable them unto all holy obedience, as the evidence of the truth of their faith and thankfulness to God, and as the way which he hath appointed them to salvation.

The Lord Jesus, by His perfect obedience, and sacrifice of himself, which He, through the eternal Spirit, once offered up unto God, hath fully satisfied the justice of his Father; and purchased, not only reconciliation, but an everlasting inheritance in the kingdom of heaven, for all those whom the Father hath given unto him (Jn 6:37). Although the work of redemption was not actually wrought by Christ till after his incarnation, yet the virtue, efficacy, and benefits thereof were communicated unto the elect, in all ages successively from the beginning of the world, in and by those promises, types and sacrifices, wherein he was revealed, and signified to be the seed of the woman which should bruise the serpent's head; and the Lamb slain from the beginning of the world; being yesterday and today the same, and forever.

Christ, the King – Christ executes the office of a King, in calling out of the world a people to Himself, and giving them officers, laws, and censures, by which He visibly governs them; in bestowing saving grace upon His elect, rewarding their obedience, and correcting them for their sins, preserving and supporting them under all their temptations and sufferings, restraining and overcoming all their enemies, and powerfully ordering all things for His own glory, and their good; and also in taking vengeance on the rest, who know not God, and obey not the gospel.

The Suffering Servant

Nowhere in all the OT is the gospel of Jesus Christ portrayed more clearly than in Isaiah 53. Some seven hundred years before the Son of God came into the world, God opened the eyes of his prophet Isaiah to envision the mediatorial saving work of the Messiah, God's Suffering Servant. The Suffering Servant of Isaiah 53 is Jesus Christ, the Son of God, who bore our griefs and carried our sorrows, and bore the sin of many, and made intercession for the transgressors (Is 53:4, 12). Leading up to the soteriological summit of Isaiah 53, the prophet envisions three previous suffering servant songs: Isaiah 42:1-4; 49:1-6; 50:4-9;

and 52:13-53:12.1 This essay will explain how the Four Songs of the Suffering Servant proleptically portray both the Person and work of the Messiah as well as the work the Messiah accomplishes through His empowered suffering servants.

The term "servant" *ebed* עֶבֶד occurs some forty times in the Book of Isaiah. Beginning with Isaiah 41:8, the nation of Israel is referred at least nine times to as the Lord's "servant." In the other occurrences, "the servant refers to a righteous individual within the nation who serves the nation."[2] While there is a certain degree of ambiguity in some passages as to whether it is the nation or an individual (cf. 44:1–2), in the prophecy in Isaiah 52:13–53:12, the individual nature of the servant is pronounced.

The four songs of the Suffering Servant were first identified by Bernhard Duhm in his 1892 commentary on Isaiah. As to the identity of the individual servant in these songs, there are a few views. One critical view, understands the servant to be a borrowed substitute king motif from ANE sources. For some, the servant refers to the exiles who return from the exile. For others, what is envisioned in the songs are the prophetic experience of the prophets in the OT.

Regarding the Jewish interpretation, messianic interpretations have not become predominant, rather Isaiah 53 is interpreted as the nation of Israel as a whole or the righteous within the nation.[3] However, this cannot be so as Walt Kaiser observes "because the

---

[1] Some regard Isaiah 61:1-3 as a fifth servant song.

[2] Darrell L. Bock and Mitch Glaser, *The Gospel According to Isaiah 53: Encountering the Suffering Servant in Jewish and Christian Theology* (Grand Rapids, MI: Kregel, 2012), 111.

[3] Ibid., 64.

Lord makes his [the servant's] life a guilt [אָשָׁם] offering."[4]

Another sees the individual servant as King Jehoiachin who suffered exile. Still, there are even mythical or cultic interpretations. However, the singular "my servant" can have three legitimate Christian uses. First, it can refer to Israel as God's servant people, or second, more specifically, to some part of the nation—a remnant group within Israel, and third, it can refer to a single Servant who suffers vicariously as an Israelite for true Israel, the righteous remnant, as well as for those who will turn to him from the nations.[5]

As regard to mission, the corporate mission of the servants is to do the will of God to accomplish God's righteous purposes in the earth (Is 41:8-9, 15-16). As God's Elect Servant, His mission was to take up the failed mission of Israel, to settle a true judgment that Yahweh alone is to be worshipped, to reveal God's Law, and establish God's just order (the Kingdom). Called to the office of a Mediator to be Prophet, Priest, and King, to be the Savior and Redeemer of men, the Servant did not assume this to Himself, but was called of His Father.

Considering the relationship between the Messiah and the Servant in Isaiah one need look no further than Isaiah 53 where the mission of the individual Servant is given its fullest exposition in Isaiah 52:13–53:12. What remains to be seen is the relationship between the individual Servant and the corporate servants.

---

[4] Ibid., 92.
[5] Ibid.

How the Servant is Portrayed in the NT

In the NT, Jesus clearly saw Himself as the prophesied Servant of Isaiah 53 and is clearly portrayed as such by the NT authors who both quote and allude to the wording or concepts of Isaiah 53 at least fifty times, and directly quote seven times.[6] In Matthew's gospel, Jesus comes as the suffering servant, identifying with the sinful humanity he came to save. In fulfilment of the second song, "He has made My mouth like a sharp sword" (Is 49:2), Jesus is the One through whom God's righteous purpose is finally accomplished in that He calls sinners to repentance (Mt 9:13), bring division (Mt 10:34), gathers the lost sheep of Israel (Mt 15:24; 18:11).

As the Servant, the Son of God is made man (Mt 1:23), submits to baptism (Mt 3:15), perfectly fulfills the righteous requirements of the law (Mt 5:17), delivers His people from supernatural bondage (Mt 8:14-17), dies a cruel death as a common criminal as the substitute in His people's place (Mt 26:67; 27:35), by which He brings an unexpected salvation to all peoples (Mt 3:15; 28:19).

In the other three gospels, Jesus is likewise clearly portrayed as the Suffering Servant of Isaiah 53. In John's gospel, in a manner reminiscent of Isaiah 42:1, John the Baptist declares: "Behold! The Lamb of God who takes away the sin of the world (Jn 1:29)! In John 12:37-41, the author quotes Isaiah 53:1 and applies it to Jesus: "But though he had done so many miracles before them, yet they believed not on him." In perhaps

---

[6] Ibid., 113. Direct quotations include: Matthew 8:14-17; John 12:37-41; Luke 22:35-38; 1 Peter 2:19-25; Acts 8:26-35; Romans 10:11-21.

the clearest, direct citation from Isaiah 53, Jesus identified Himself as the sacrificial lamb, whose blood of the covenant is poured out for many (Mk 14:24).[7]

In the rest of the Bible, Jesus is likewise clearly shown to be Isaiah's Servant. For example, in the Book of Acts, Jesus is referred to as the servant of God and the righteous One (Acts 3:13-14). And in a clear citation of Isaiah 53:7–8, Acts 8 has Philip explain Jesus' life and mission to the Ethiopian eunuch (Acts 8:30-35). Then in Acts 10, Peter declares Jesus the Servant preached "good news of peace," a clear reference to Isaiah 52:7.

In Romans chapter 10, the Apostle Paul employs quotations from the Book of Isaiah to demonstrate how Israel's unbelief has opened the door to the blessing of the Gentiles (Rom 10:16). In Peter's epistles, he quotes various parts of Isaiah 53 and applies them to the Lord Jesus. For example, in 1 Peter 3:18 he declares: "For Christ also suffered once for sins, the just for the unjust, that He might bring us to God, being put to death in the flesh but made alive by the Spirit."

In the NT, Jesus is clearly portrayed as the Isaianic Servant. As the Prophet, He reveals God's will for the salvation of men (Jn 6:40), renders a judgment that God alone is to be worshipped. As Priest, He reveals the character and nature of God by sacrificing Himself for His people, and as King, restores the covenant by inaugurating His Kingdom (Dan 2:34-35, 44; 7:14; Rev 1:5). In these ways, the NT canvases the broad scope and meaning of Isaiah's Suffering Servant and how it corresponds to Jesus Christ, the Messiah, who is True Israel (Mt 2:15).

---

[7] Ibid., 95.

The Relationship Between the Corporate and Individual Servant

Jesus said it is enough for a disciple to be like His teacher, and a servant to be like His master (Mt 10:25). In the NT, the authors demonstrate both the individual and corporate nature of the servant and the way they do this is they show how the work of the Suffering Servant is taken up by the suffering servants. The Spirit of Christ ruling in His servants empowers their testimony (Acts 16:7; Rev 12:11).

In the Book of Acts Paul declares: "For so the Lord has commanded us: 'I have set you as a light to the Gentiles, that you should be for salvation to the ends of the earth'" (Acts 13:47). Here Paul directly quotes Isaiah 49:6 which speaks directly of the mission of the Suffering Servant and applies it now to his own mission. This clearly demonstrates the relationship between the corporate and individual servant; the work of the Servant is being accomplished through His empowered suffering servants.

As the NT demonstrates, God's purpose of raising up the ruined posterity of Adam was accomplished by Jesus the Suffering Servant, and is now being completed through the followers of Jesus, the suffering servants (Mt 5:12; 10:19-20). Jesus told His disciples, "you shall receive power when the Holy Spirit has come upon you; and you shall be witnesses to Me in Jerusalem, and in all Judea and Samaria, and to the end of the earth" (Acts 1:8). Jesus said, you will testify to My saving work. In this way, the Servant completes His task through His empowered suffering servants who "fill up what is lacking in the afflictions of Christ, for the sake of His body, which is the church" (Col

1:24). C.S. Lewis puts it this way: "The sacrifice of Christ is repeated, or re-echoed, among His followers in varying degrees, from the cruelest martyrdom down to a self-submission of intention."[8]

The Suffering Servant of Isaiah 53 is Jesus Christ, who bore our griefs and carried our sorrows, and bore the sin of many, and made intercession for the transgressors (Is 53:4, 12). The resulting work of the Suffering Servant is many servants are raised up (Is 54). And as the corporate person of Christ, Christians are suffering servants, living out the righteousness of Jesus, being His hands and feet, proclaiming the gospel, and suffering as He did for the sake of His people until they all come in (Col 1:24-29).

The Person and Work of the Holy Spirit

Previously we have discussed the truth of God's triune nature, that He is three Persons within the unity of a single divine Being. God the Father represents the Trinity. In His unique relationship to the Son of God, the Father determined before eternity to send His Son to redeem His elect. In His unique relationship to the Holy Spirit, the Father sends the Holy Spirit to effectually call and apply the eternal salvation purchased by the Son. As the third Person of the trinity, like the Son, the Holy Spirit is co-substantial and co-eternal with the Father.

The Holy Spirit, eternally proceeding from the Father and the Son, through the ministry of regeneration and progressive sanctification applies

---

[8] C.S. Lewis, *The Problem of Pain* (New York: Harper Row, 1960), 104.

salvation, guides and comforts the children of God, directs and empowers the church in fulfilment of the Great commission, and convicts the world of sin, righteousness, and judgment. Thus, as Wayne Grudem rightly observes:

> The work of the Holy Spirit is to manifest the active presence of God in the world, and especially in the church.[9]

Specifically, the work of the Holy Spirit is:

1. He gives life (Ps 104:30), and new life (Jn 3:6-7).
2. He gives power for service (1 Sam 16:13; Acts 1:8).
3. He purifies (Mt 3:11; Lk 3:16).
4. He reveals truth (Zech 7:12; Jn 16:13).
5. He convicts the world of sin (Jn
6. He gives evidence of God's presence (Acts 5:32).
7. He guides and directs God's people (Acts 8:29).
8. He gives believers assurance (Rom 8:16; 1 Jn 4:13).
9. He teaches and illuminates (Jn 14:26).
10. He unifies (Acts 2:41-42).

At the moment of regeneration, the Holy Spirit cultivates Christian character, comforts believers, and bestows spiritual gifts by which they serve God through His church. He seals the believer unto the day of final redemption. His presence in the Christian is the guarantee that God will bring the believer into the fullness of the stature of Christ.

Without the Holy Spirit, the Church can do nothing. As the Lord and Giver of life, the Holy Spirit created the

---

[9] Wayne Grudem, *Systematic Theology: An Introduction to Biblical Doctrine* (Grand Rapids, MI: Zondervan, 1994), 634.

Church, raises up God's people from ruin, disposes gifts, raises up leaders, guides, directs, convicts, comforts, etc.

In Romans 6, the Apostle Paul teaches us as Christians we are going to cultivate some type of fruit, either good or bad, either unto righteous or unrighteous, as we are led either by our own sin nature (old man) or led by the Spirit. The Spirit is willing to lead us in bearing fruit to God but the flesh is weak. As pastors, we are to die to the old man every day and bear fruit for God. This is the challenge the Bible lays down: if you desire to live a godly life in Christ you will undoubtedly be at war.

God's desire is for His people to live more and more for Him. The Holy Spirit plants the spiritual root of eternal life in believers, so that by His grace they may bear fruit unto holiness. Living by the Spirit is the root, walking by the Spirit is the fruit (Gal 5).

In Galatians 6, the Apostle Paul has much to teach us regarding the mission of the Holy Spirit and how believers are to keep in step with Him. I Galatians 5:16, Paul writes: "Walk in the Spirit, and you shall not fulfill the lust of the flesh." Walking by the Spirit means living moment by moment submissively trusting in the Holy Spirit rather than in self. Paul is speaking to believers. If you're not born again, all you'll be able to do is fulfill the desires and lusts of the flesh.

This says so much of the mission of the Holy Spirit. We are to walk by the Spirit. The apostle uses the metaphor of walking. The idea is if you keep walking, you will certainly cover spiritual ground and eventually reach the destination. For the apostle, walking was an apt metaphor. If any believer was walking, that believer was going somewhere. And in the Christian life we are either walking or we're stalled; sanctification is measurable. We are to keep in step with the Spirit.

No one has ever been saved without the Holy Spirit's work. In the Old Testament, the work of the Holy Spirit was the same in kind albeit less in degree. For example, in Numbers 11, the Lord "took of the Spirit that was upon" Moses and "placed the same upon the seventy elders" who prophesied in the camp of Israel (Num 11:25-28). And Moses said, "Oh, that all of Lord's people were prophets and that the Lord would put His Spirit upon them" (Num 11:30)! Then on the Day of Pentecost this prophetic prayer of Moses was fulfilled when God poured out His Spirit and empowered His church to turn the world upside down. God's people are now prophetic, "not in a technical sense of giving revelation," but in the sense of forthtelling the saving truths of God who gave His Son Jesus Christ for the redemption of believing sinners.[10]

Pastors are called to make disciples who make disciples. Christian pastors are to teach and demonstrate through life witness the fact that holiness is not a matter of painstaking conformity to the external law code. Instead, they are to show that holiness is a question of the Holy Spirit's producing His fruit in the life of the one He has regenerated. The Spirit provides us the power and the motivation to do what God requires; what God commands He gives. It's impossible to obey God's commandments and fulfill them in the manner which pleases Him without the power He supplies. This is what the Holy Spirit provides. We are to keep in step with Him.

---

[10] Paul Pettit, *Foundations of Spiritual Formation: A Community Approach to Becoming Like Christ* (Grand Rapids: Kregel Academic, 2008), 114.

Chapter Seven: Doctrine of Salvation

"Thou hast made us for thyself, O Lord, and our heart is restless until it finds its rest in thee." – Augustine

One's view of humanity effects how everything is seen; especially a need to be saved. So far, we have made an effort to demonstrate man's fallenness and need of grace. As it has been said, according to the Christian world view, man is dead in his trespasses and sins, defiled in nature, and under the condemning wrath of God. And this is how man will remain unless Christ's redemption is applied to him (Jn 3:36).

Our purpose in this chapter will be to discuss the nature of salvation as it is revealed in the Bible. Scripture speaks of salvation in terms of the Father giving a people to the Son (Jn 6:39; Eph. 1:4–12), the Son accomplishing that plan by his life and death (Jn 6:37–40; 10:14–18; Heb. 10:5–18), and the Spirit's work to bring those same people to faith and union in Christ (Rom. 8:29–30; Eph. 1:11–13; 1 Pet. 1:5). See figure 7-1 below.

As has been said, according to the Bible, everyone belongs to one of either two covenants, that of Adam and the covenant of works (Rom 5:12), or of Christ, the second Adam, and the covenant of grace (Rom 5:15-21). Believers are therefore saved by grace alone through faith and brought into the covenant of grace by the working of the Holy Spirit (Eph 2:8-10).

Salvation therefore consists of the remission of sins, the impartation of the righteousness of Jesus Christ, the gift of eternal life and the blessings that accompany it. Salvation is a free gift of God and is received by grace alone through faith alone apart from human works of merit. Even the ability to believe is a gift from God. This blessing in no way relieves men of their responsibility to repent and believe. Scripture clearly teaches both the divine sovereignty of God in election and His divine summons to repent and believe in Christ for salvation.

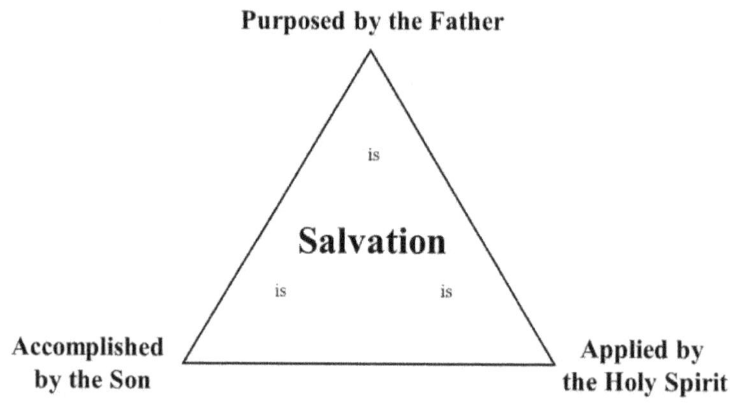

Figure 7-1 Salvation.

Election is another word that is used in conjunction with salvation. Election is the gracious purpose of God, according to which He regenerates, justifies, sanctifies, and glorifies sinners. It is the glorious display of God's sovereign goodness, and is infinitely wise, holy, and unchangeable. It excludes boasting and promotes humility. All true believers endure to the end. They, whom God has accepted in His Beloved, effectually called, and sanctified by His Spirit, can neither totally nor finally fall away from the state of grace, but shall certainly persevere therein to the end, and be eternally saved (Heb 7:25).

Grace and faith are two more words used when discussing salvation. Grace is the unmerited favor of God, and faith is the relational response to God's promises. Faith is also the work of God in our hearts, which saves us (Luke 7:50), guides us (2 Cor 5:7), heals us (Luke 8:48) and transforms us (2 Pet 3:18). And so, faith is God's way of bringing us to Himself. The gospel is therefore God's restoration program for mankind, who are fallen in Adam's physical and spiritual death, but by grace through faith are raised in Christ's resurrection, first spiritually, then physically (Jn 5:25-29; 1 Pet 1:3; 2 Pet 3:10).

When a man is born again, he receives a renewed mind, will, and emotions. Conversion is the word we use to describe this action of God. And yet, another word used in conjunction with salvation is justification. God's justification of a sinner is based upon the obedience and righteousness of Christ alone which He "accounts" or "credits" to the believing sinner as his own. Whereas, in Adam all die because they receive his imputed sin, in Christ, all live, by grace through faith, and receive His imputed righteousness (Rom 4).[1]

This righteousness of Christ, the believing sinner receives, and is accounted "just" or "righteous," in the sight of God. This is, as Martin Luther put it, the article of a standing or falling church. Augustine writes, "Since in the first man, the whole human race fell under condemnation, those vessels which are made of it unto honor are not vessels of self-righteousness, but divine

---

[1] Romans 4 declares sinners justified before God on the basis of the imputed righteousness of Christ, and uses the word we translate "accounted" no less than 11 times.

mercy. When other vessels are made unto dishonor, it must be imputed not to injustice, but to judgment."[2]

God is Love incarnate. His solution to our predicament, is one in which He decrees to save by One whom He will raise up to David, the Lord our righteousness, Jesus Christ (Jer 23:5-6). Justification is therefore, a legal, forensic declaration of God, and is used in Scripture to denote the acceptance of believers as righteous in the sight of God on account of the perfect finished work of God's Son, Jesus Christ.

The reformer John Calvin rightly called justification the principal hinge by which religion is supported, the soil out of which the Christian life develops, and the substance of piety. The righteousness of God is *God's incarnate obedience*, an act of God in human nature fulfilling the covenant from man's side.

So, any view which states that our faith is counted as righteousness is a misunderstanding of the whole council of God. For example, the apostle James demonstrates in James chapter two how believers are justified before observing men to be Christians, by saying that "a man is justified by works, and not by faith only" (Jam 2:24). But certainly, this is not to be understood of one being justified in the sense as made in right standing with God, for this would contradict the apostle Paul, as well as the rest of Scripture, who states in no uncertain terms, that such righteousness is theoretically possible, though practically impossible (Rom 2:17-24). James' use of justified in verse 24 seems to go along with the "show me", of verse 18. It seems James in chapter two is merely saying

[2] Augustine, Epistle 106, *De Praedestinationae et Gratia*, as quoted in Institutes of the Christian Religion, III.23.11, 632.

Abraham's works of faith demonstrated, among men, his justifying faith in God. John Gill observes, "Abraham, in offering up his son, was a clear proof of the truth of his faith, there commended: by this it was made known what a strong faith he had in God, and what reason there was to believe that he was a justified person."[3]

The point is, justification is the Father's legal decree, based on the Son's accomplished righteousness, as it is applied by the life-living Spirit. Our sins were the judicial ground of the sufferings of Christ, so that they were a satisfaction of justice; and his righteousness is the judicial ground of our acceptance with God, so that our pardon is an act of justice.[4]

We would do well to note an important distinction between justification, God's accounting believers as righteous and sanctification, God's process of making his saints like His Son Jesus. In other words, while justification is once for all, sanctification is God's process of making His people holy and separate. Sanctification is the daily putting on of the new man in Christ and dying to ourselves (2 Cor 5:17; Eph 4:20-24; Col 3:8-11). It is a walk of faith (2 Cor 5:7), relying on the grace of God to strengthen us in our weaknesses.

God is Love incarnate, His solution to our predicament is Jesus Christ, the Lamb of God (Jn 1:29). God imputes righteousness to us and sees us in Christ. As Doug Kelly states, "The doctrine of justification by faith, is the article of a standing or falling church."[5] Justification constitutes the only escape from the wrath of God (Jn 3:36). Sinners escape

---

3 Gill, Exposition of the Whole Bible, James 2:24.

4 Hodge, An Exposition of the Second Letter to the Corinthians, 150.

5 Kelly, The True Church, 11.

the coming wrath of God by being accounted righteous by virtue of Christ's all-sufficient righteousness imputed to them (1 Thess 1:10). Thus, the righteousness of God is God's incarnate obedience.

Jesus uses a parable, the Pharisee and the tax collector, to demonstrate the impiety of self-righteousness in Luke 18:9-14. Jesus tells us, "Two men went up to the temple to pray, one a Pharisee and the other a tax collector" (Lk 18:11). The proud Pharisee's prayer, more of a pompous declaration, appealed to his own perceived self-righteousness by asserting, "God, I thank You that I am not like other men." The self-righteous Pharisee no doubt had the tax collector in mind, and "informs" God of his "righteous deeds," whereas the tax collector, painfully aware of his own unworthiness, beat his chest and cried "God, be merciful to me a sinner!" and appealed to God's sense of grace.

Jesus tells us that it was the tax collector, not the Pharisee, "who went down to his house justified" (Lk 18:14). Man will be vindicated, accounted "righteous" and justified solely on the grounds of his identification with Christ and His righteous. Any self-righteous is viewed as detestable in God's sight. Jesus told the Pharisees, "You are those who justify yourselves before men, but God knows your hearts. For what is highly esteemed among men is an abomination in the sight of God" (Lk 16:15).

Legalism is depending on one's own efforts toward righteousness rather than the righteousness that God accounts to us in Jesus Christ. The natural man desires to make himself acceptable before God by his fulfilling of the requirements of the law. The Bible tells us that this is an impossibility (Is 64:6; Rom 3:20; Gal 2:16;

3:11), however, God gives us the good news of the gospel that while we were yet sinners Christ died for us, so that whoever believes in Him might become the righteousness of God (Rom 5:8; 2 Cor 5:21).

John Wesley, the great evangelist and co-founder of the Methodist movement, before his 'Aldersgate experience' was a mere moralist.[6] He had been ordained as a minister in the Church of England but lacked saving faith. His religion consisted in earnestly striving to keep the commandments; it was void of the assurance of salvation that comes from relying on Christ's righteousness and not our own.[7] Then one evening at a prayer meeting on Aldersgate Street in London, while Wesley heard Luther's Preface to Romans being read, he recounts, "I felt strangely warmed, and I felt I did trust in Christ, Christ alone for salvation, and an assurance was given to me that He had taken away my sins, even mine, and saved me from the law of sin and death."[8] After his conversion Wesley's indefatigable evangelistic work began; work for which the world will never be the same.

At the moment of regeneration, the Spirit cultivates Christian character, comforts believers, and bestows spiritual gifts by which they serve God through His church. He seals the believer unto the day of final redemption. His presence in the Christian is the guarantee that God will bring the believer into the fullness of the stature of Christ.

---

[6] John Wesley (1703-1791) was an evangelist and theologian of the Church of England, who, along with George Whitefield, was instrumental in the First Great Awakening.

[7] Bloesch, Faith and It's Counterfeits, 107.

[8] Outler, John Wesley, 66.

Chapter Eight: Doctrine of the Church

"There must be sleep in the first Adam before God can take out of him the ordained spouse. And there must be death in the second Adam before God can take out of Him the chosen bride." – Horatius Bonar

A pastor is a gift to the church (Eph 4:11). The Church as the Body of Christ, from both the Old and New Testament periods, includes all of the redeemed of all the ages, believers from every tribe, and tongue, and people, and nation. The church consists of those called out of the world by the Father, redeemed by the Son, and saved and brought into a covenant fellowship with God by the Holy Spirit. The church is therefore not an aside or parenthesis in God's redemptive plan, it is God's only saving program for mankind (Rev 7:9).

Over against any assertion of a 'race based' salvation, Christ declares: "Do not suppose that you can say to yourselves, 'We have Abraham for our father'; for I say to you, that God is able from these stones to raise up children to Abraham" (Matt 3:9). Grace does not run in the blood; God's children are "born not of blood, nor of the will of the flesh, nor of the will of man, but of God" (Jn 1:12-13; 3:3).

The story of the church, however, begins with Israel, the Old Testament people of God. As James Montgomery Boice observes:

> Strictly speaking, the church is the creation of the historical Christ and therefore dates from the time of

> Christ. But the church has roots in the Old Testament and cannot be understood well without that background. This is true theologically because the idea of a called-out "people of God" obviously existed in the Old Testament period, just as in the New.[1]

As has been said, God created everything that exists *ex nihilo,* that is out of nothing. He created mankind from one man and one woman while setting aside for Himself a particular people for His very own (Titus 2:14). The church is therefore God's covenant community, God's visible witness, and God's instrument (See figure 6-1).

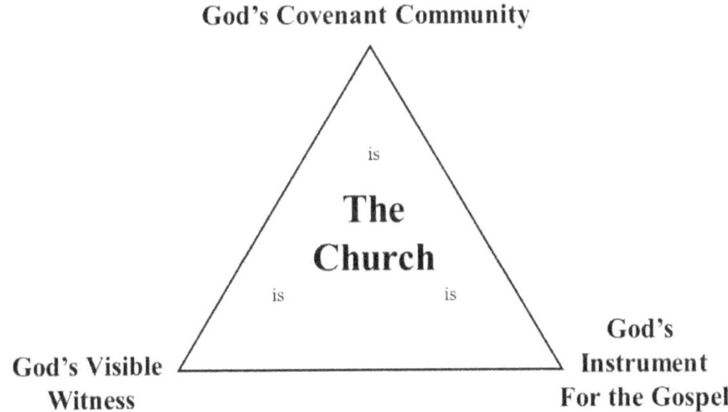

Figure 6-1. The Church.

God's Covenant Community

God created the church to be His covenant community in which He Himself dwells with His

[1] James M. Boice, Foundations of the Christian Faith, 566.

adopted children (Lev 26:11; Eph 1:5; 2:19-22). The church is the 'called out' ones, from the Greek *ekklésia* ἐκκλησία, a conjugation of two words "ek" meaning "out from" and "kaleo" meaning "called." The Hebrew qahal קָהָל, an assembly gathered together for a solemn ceremony (Dt 9:10), is the Old Testament Masoretic Text equivalent to ekklésia.[2]

An important distinction pastors are to teach is this: Old Testament saints were saved in the same way as believers today, by grace through faith (Gen 15:6; Rom 4:5). There is much confusion in the church today regarding this. However, the Bible teaches the only way believers have ever been saved is by grace alone through faith alone (Gen 15:6; Gal 3:9; Heb 13:8).

The way the Bible explains this in the Book of Hebrews is this: The saints of old looked forward to the saving work of Christ in and through those types which foreshadowed the redeeming work that He would do (Heb 11:25-26; Gal 4:4). When the OT saints died, they were ushered into the saving presence of God because of the saving work that the Son of God would accomplish in the fulness of time on their behalf (Rom 3:25; Gal 3:9). The church therefore consists of the full number of God's people of "all nations, tribes, peoples, and tongues," and is founded on the Person and work of Christ (Rev 7:9). Thus, there are but one people of God that have been, are, or shall be gathered into one, under Christ, and is the bride, the body, and fullness of

---

[2] The LXX, Septuagint, the 3rd Century BC Greek translation of the Hebrew Old Testament, always translates *qahal* as ekklésia which is used 80 times in the Canonical Septuagint Books. Dt 23:2 translates *qahal Yahweh* as ekklēsia Kyriou, the church of the Lord. The Masoretic Text is the God-breathed Hebrew text of the Old Testament.

Christ (Dt 9:10; Jn 10:16; Eph 1:22; 5:25-32; 1 Tim 3:15).

There are, however, marked contrasts between the old and new covenants. As we have discussed, this presupposes a covenant of grace and a covenant of works. God made a covenant of grace with Abraham and his Seed (Gen 15; Gal 3:16). This was before God gave the law to Moses. In Genesis 15, we find the promise of the Seed appearing again (Gen 3:15). And so, in the progress of redemption, God is going to create the woman Israel out of the man Abraham.

God is going to create His very Own nation out of one man. And out of this man Abraham, One is going to come forth, that is the Seed of the Woman, who is going to right the wrong, He'll crush the head of the serpent and in so doing set things right and He's going to actually be the means of the blessing of the nations.

God had already spoken to Abraham and revealed Himself and told him to leave Ur of the Chaldees. In Genesis 12:1-3, God said to Abram:

> Get out of your country, from your family and from your father's house, to a land that I will show you. 2 I will make you a great nation; I will bless you and make your name great; and you shall be a blessing. 3 I will bless those who bless you, and I will curse him who curses you; and in you all the families of the earth shall be blessed.

Essentially, there are three distinct but related promises that God made to Abraham: A seed, a land, and a universal blessing. In these words, God made an explicit promise to Abraham, and the blessing of the whole of humanity depended on that promise.

In the context of Genesis 15 Abraham is eighty-five. God called him when he was seventy-five years old. Since that time there was still no tangible evidence of God's promise. God's Word then comes to him and is aimed at his fears: '"After these things the word of the Lord came to Abram in a vision, saying, "Do not be afraid, Abram. I am your shield, your exceedingly great reward"' (Gen 15:1). God gives Abram two reasons not to fear. The first is that He Himself will be Abram's shield. God will protect him. With God as his shield, Abram has nothing to fear.

Secondly, God promised not merely to give Abram a reward but to be Abram's reward. Likewise, to those of faith, God says, I Am your inheritance, and you are mine. But this hasn't sunk in yet, and Abram is thinking, Lord, you said You were going to make of me a great nation, and that takes descendants. And as of right now, I have none. And so, in Gen 15:2, Abram says, "Lord God, what will You give me, seeing I go childless, and the heir of my house is Eliezer of Damascus?" In other words, my only heir is a Syrian slave. Abram rightly knew that God's covenant promises were dependent upon God's provision of a seed.

Right then and there, the Lord spoke into Abram's crisis of faith and reaffirmed His promise to him. The Lord takes Abram outside into the night sky and uses the stars as an illustration and said: "This one shall not be your heir, but one who will come from your own body shall be your heir. Look now toward heaven, and count the stars if you are able to number them." Abram was looking for a tangible sign of God's promise and God gave him one to create faith in him. God uses the stars as an illustration of the spiritual promises that

He has made to him, and says: "So shall your descendants be."

Then, in Gen 15:6, we witness Abram's faith and God's imputation: "And he believed in the Lord, and He accounted it to him for righteousness." This is, of course, is the passage that the Apostle Paul uses to prove the doctrine of justification by faith alone in Romans 4. There was no law as of yet. There was no sacrificial system, no circumcision. Abram hadn't done anything to earn God's favor. No deeds of righteousness. He simply trusted in what God had said, and God accounted to him righteousness, that is, right standing with Him. And as, we look at Abram, we find him to be the quintessential believer.

Abraham was called to go out. God was calling him to a life of things unseen (Heb 11). And he believed, and God credited to him as righteousness. In Galatians 3:7-9, the Apostle Paul showcases Abraham's faith as the pattern for all believers:

> 7 Therefore know that only those who are of faith are sons of Abraham. 8 And the Scripture, foreseeing that God would justify the Gentiles by faith, preached the gospel to Abraham beforehand, saying, "In you all the nations shall be blessed." 9 So then those who are of faith are blessed with believing Abraham.

Abraham is the father of all who believe because he staked his life, death, and all eternity on what God had said. He believed God, in spite of how things seemed at the time. And that is certainly the challenge for all believers. The point is, the church consists of those who like Abraham have been called out of the world to leave behind familiar, safe and secure things to follow God in a life which is often full of uncertainty. Likewise, believers are called to put behind them their own worldly agenda and world view and adopt the Lord's plan.

God made the promise to Abram and his faith rose out of the darkness of his doubts and fears. Then, in Gen 15:7, God assured him of His promise of the seed and said: "I am the Lord, who brought you out of Ur of the Chaldeans, to give you this land to inherit it." And though Abram believed God, he sought further assurance. And in v. 8, he says: "Lord God, how shall I know that I will inherit it?" And to assure Abram, God cuts a covenant with him and confirms His promise by a blood sign.

As we have surveyed Genesis one and two, we were introduced to the word covenant. We found that a covenant is a special relationship established by God that has both blessings and obligations. O. Palmer Robertson succinctly defines a covenant as: "A bond in blood, sovereignly administered." A covenant is therefore a mutual relationship that is binding, that is, it's for life, like marriage. And it is one which comes with mutual blessings and mutual obligations.

What is amazing is how this covenant is ratified. God has Abram prepare various animals for sacrifice. The Lord said to him: "Bring Me a three-year-old heifer, a three-year-old female goat, a three-year-old ram, a turtledove, and a young pigeon" (Gen 15:9). Interestingly, all five of these animals were later to be used in the five Levitical sacrifices God gave Moses (the burnt offering, the grain offering, the peace offering, the sin offering, and the guilt offering). Each of these five animals gathered by Abram are individually connected to one of these specific offerings.

What does this mean? As each of these sacrifices point to Christ, it means ultimately, the way all of God's promises will be realized is in and through Christ's once for all sacrifice. This verse also has much to commend to us about the life of faith. Abram is told to do something and he simply trusts and obeys God. Sure, Abram had concerns about how this was all going to pan out, after all, he is just a man. He doesn't know how this will all come about, but he believes anyway and obeys in every detail.

Abram was familiar with the particular customs and rituals of those days. In the Ancient Near East, when tribes or nations came into conflict and one overlord or king conquered another tribe, as an act of loyalty, the king or the overlord would have the conquered peoples walk between the pieces of slaughtered animals. This would symbolize as long as you are obedient and loyal to me, I will protect you, I will provide you a system of justice, and I will be one who blesses you. But if you rebel against me, be it done to you as we have done to these animals; may you be slaughtered, even as we have slaughtered these animals.

In other words, walking between the pieces of animals was an oath of self-curse or of self-destruction. No doubt being familiar with this ritual, Abram we are told in Gen 15:10, "brought all these to Him and cut them in Two, down the middle, and placed each piece opposite the other; but he did not cut the birds in two." Then Abram waited. And as Gen 15:11-16 tell us, when the vultures came down on the carcasses, Abram drove them away. And as the sun was setting, a deep sleep fell upon Abram: "and behold, horror and great darkness fell upon him." Then God said to Abram: "Know certainly that your descendants will be strangers in a land that is not theirs, and will serve them, and they will afflict them four hundred years. And also the nation whom they serve I will judge; afterward they shall come out with great possessions. Now as for you, you shall go to your fathers in peace; you shall be buried at a good old age. But in the fourth generation they shall return here, for the iniquity of the Amorites is not yet complete."

Then, something amazing happens in Gen 15:17, "And it came to pass, when the sun went down and it was dark, that behold, there appeared a smoking oven and a burning torch that passed between those pieces." This was God's way of ratifying His covenant He made with Abraham. It reveals at least three main things: A prophecy, a sign and a foreshadowing.

First, it is a prophecy. The time will come when Abraham descendants will be strangers in a land not theirs. This is Egypt. There they will be slaves to the Egyptians, who will afflict them four hundred years. But Egypt will be judged for this and Abraham's people, who will then be called Israel, will plunder the Egyptians and come out with great possessions. God also graciously tells Abram that he will be buried at a good old age. And then, notice, as touching the promise of the land, God says in effect that He will clear out the land for His people. And what's hinted at, is God's people will themselves be the very instrument of judgment.

One thing this passage also shows, is God has a predetermined limit to which He allows nations to go in their sin before He steps in and judges them. There's a point where enough is enough. God's great patience was demonstrated in waiting those 400 years. As Psalm 145:8 declares: "The Lord is gracious and full of compassion, slow to anger and great in mercy." But when His patience does not meet the repentance of sinners, there can be only wrath and judgment.

Then, in Gen 15:18-21, God declares that He would dispossess ten nations in Canaan in order to make a special land for His people. And He later did just that as this promise of land was literally fulfilled under Israel's leaders Joshua and then David. In fact, when Solomon comes to the throne and dedicates the temple, he says this regarding the land promise in 1 Kings 8:56: "Blessed be the Lord, who has given rest to His people Israel, according to all that He promised. There has not failed one word of all His good promise, which He promised through His servant Moses."

What we need to understand, when we look to the land promise, as the NT clarifies, God's promise made to Abraham and his seed was a promise that he should inherit the world, as the Apostle Paul declares in Rom 4:13: Paul writes: "For the promise that he would be the heir of the world was not to Abraham or to his seed through the law, but through the righteousness of faith." What this means is the real estate in the Middle East is not the be all and end all.

The Promised Land served as a type of God's promised rest. That is something Hebrews chapter 4 teaches us. Long after the entrance into the Promised Land was achieved under Joshua, David spoke in Psalm 95 of a rest that may be entered or missed. In other words, the Bible teaches us God's rest has both a spatial and temporal relation – that is, God's rest includes both time and space. And the place of God's rest is God's presence as Exodus 33:14 tells us. The Lord declares: "My presence will go with you, and I will give you rest."

So, what is God's rest? It's where He is. God's presence is rest. God promises Abram a great inheritance, which over time would become more specific with later revelation. When we look at the life of Abraham, we begin to understand what the inheritance really is. God says inheritance is the son of promise, the inheritance is the place of promise and the inheritance is the people of promise. In other words, God promises Abram a son, a place, and a people – as numerous as the stars in the heavens. And the people themselves are the place of God's rest and the place of God's inheritance.

It is for this reason then in Hebrews 11:8-10, the apostle tells us: "By faith Abraham obeyed when he was called to go out to the place which he would receive as an inheritance. And he went out, not knowing where he was going. 9 By faith he dwelt in the land of promise as in a foreign country, dwelling in tents with Isaac and Jacob, the heirs with him of the same promise; 10 for he waited for the city which has foundations, whose builder and maker is God."

With this understanding, Palestine was but a predictive type. In the NT, the apostles give us the inspired interpretation of the land promise and show us that the land concept is expanded to include the universe. And so, our inheritance, that is all believers, who are sons and daughters of Abraham by faith, is the new heavens and new earth. This is a classic case of the NT telling us what the OT really meant. What we learn from this is: We have to let the NT interpret the OT for us.

This also signifies that the accomplishment of this covenant will be by "a way" made through death. That is, by salvation through judgment. By this covenant ratification ceremony, God is saying the way back is through sacrifice. Also, importantly, the covenant God makes with Abraham and his seed is enacted by God alone. By passing through the animal parts alone, God was saying essentially two things: First, He says in effect, I will fulfill the stipulations of the covenant for both of us. That is, the covenant is initiated by God and completed by Him without man's help.

Here's the truly fascinating thing that we learn in Genesis 15. Abram himself does not walk between the pieces of the slaughtered animals. God in the form of a smoking oven and a burning torch, both symbols of God's glory and power, passes between the pieces while Abram is asleep. And of course, this points us to the Lord Jesus Christ, Who as God incarnate fulfills the covenant on the part of God as God and on the part of man as Man.

Secondly, God walks down the bloody path alone in order to say: Abram, I promise unto my own death that I will fulfill My covenant commitments to you. And be it done to me as we have done to these animals if I do not fulfill My covenant promises to you. And of course, that is precisely what God does in Christ when He takes the covenant curse upon Himself in order for the blessings of the covenant to be realized. The Apostle Paul gives us an inspired interpretation of this in Galatians 3 when he says that Christ became a curse by Hanging on the tree so that "in Christ Jesus the blessing of Abraham might come to the Gentiles (Gal 3:13-14).

In the progress of redemption, God's covenant with Abraham narrows our understanding of the promised Seed of the woman, the One who will crush the head of the serpent (Gen 3:15), to be also the One through whom all of God's blessings come (Gen 12; Gal 3:13-14). That in Jesus Christ, "All the families of the earth shall be blessed." Think of this, in order to honor the promise contained in this chapter, God would bring the children of Israel out of Egypt and send His Son into the world. God appointed a way for the nations to receive the promise. The promise of God is His guarantee of redemption. And the means for achieving the promise is the covenant.

Of the various aspects of the promise of God we have heard, of seed, of land, of protection and blessing, as we come to the NT, the apostles interpret all of these in one way. The Apostle John declares: "And this is the promise that He has promised us—eternal life" (1 John 2:25). In this way, believers get back the life we lost and the fellowship we lost and the righteousness we lost in Adam. Believers are reconciled to God through the cross of Jesus Christ.

Later, God gave the Law to Moses, to give Israel His standards for how they were to live the redeemed life. The Law is holy, righteous, just and good. It is the mirror of God's holy character and His righteous standard for life and faithfulness. The Old Testament believers lived their lives according to the law in order to be separate from the world and so be consecrated to God. This was in obedience to God's righteous demands for holiness. However, the Law was never intended to be the final revelation of God (Gal 3:11). The purpose of the law was never to impart life but to better lead us to the promise (Gal 3:21). What we may understand then is, the old covenant fulfilled its incomplete purpose. No one was ever saved through Law-keeping.

The new covenant, which is the Abrahamic covenant ratified, deals with mankind's two greatest problems; both of which separate us from a Holy God. The first is the problem of guilt because of sin. Jesus solves this by shedding his blood to lift our guilt by taking it on himself: "This cup is the new covenant in my blood" (Lk 22:20).

The second problem is rebellion, our tendency to run away from God and follow the destructive suggestions of the world and Satan. This God solves by writing his law on our hearts, thus making us willing and obedient; so as to comply out of love, with a heart inclined toward the Lord. This is the major difference between the old and the new covenants. Whereas the old covenant was a mixed covenant that included both those that loved the Lord like Abraham and David, as well as those who were corrupt like Ahab, all those who are members of the new covenant know the Lord savingly.

What about Israel? As the Apostle Paul teaches, believing Jews are grafted back into their own olive tree (Rom 11:24). When Jews see Jesus as the Messiah, and come to Him in faith, along with the Gentiles, they become "fellow heirs of the same body, and partakers of His promise in Christ through the gospel" (Eph 3:6). God's covenant community therefore consists of everyone God *calls* out of darkness into His marvelous light (Dt 4:20, 34; 1 Pet 2:9).

When the apostle Paul declares in Romans 11:26: "And in this way all Israel will be saved," he is referring to the completed remnant consisting of both believing Jew and Gentile, which in the apostle's present time are being gathered and will continue to be gathered in the interadvent period from "all nations, tribes, peoples, and tongues" (Rom 11:26; Rev 7:9). The point is, the future of ethnic Israel is an integral part of the current era of gospel proclamation. God has only one saving program – the church (Mt 16:18).

Israel is the wife of Yahweh; the church is the bride of Christ. It is not physical descent from Abraham that makes you part of the covenant people of God but faith in Christ. The presupposition here is that the New Testament church is the continuation of the Old Testament people of God, and as such, the *Ekklésia* or *Qahal* consists of all the redeemed of all the ages (Eph 2:19-22).

The prophet Ezekiel allegorically demonstrates God's relationship to His people in terms of a husband; Israel is presented as an unfaithful bride. "Yes, I swore an oath to you and entered into a covenant with you, and you became Mine," says the Lord God" (Ezek 16:8). But "You are an adulterous wife, who takes strangers instead of her husband" (Ezek 16:32). Therefore "I will judge you as women who break wedlock" (Ezek 16:38). The relationship between God and His people is interrupted by sin, so that God calls Israel *Lo-Ammi*, 'not my people' (Hos 1:9; Mt 21:43); but the Scripture tells, "we once were not a people but now are the people of God" (1 Pet 2:10). By the grace of God, those who were, *Lo-Ammi* 'not my people,' whether they are covenant-breaking Jews or Gentiles outside the covenant, are made the people of God and receive mercy (Hos 1:10).[3]

The Apostle Paul tells us in Eph 5:25, "Christ loved the church and gave Himself for her." According to this truth Wayne Grudem writes, "Here the term "the Church" is used to apply to all those whom Christ died

---

[3] Clowney, The Church, 29.

to redeem, all those who are saved by the death of Christ. But that must include all true believers for all time, both believers in the New Testament age and believers in the Old Testament as well. So great is God's plan for the church that He has exalted Christ to a position of highest authority for the sake of the church: "He has put all things under His feet and has made Him the head over all things *for the church*, which is His body, the fullness of Him who fills all in all" (Eph 1:22-23).[4]

The church is the messianic community; the redeemed of all the ages. It includes believers from every tribe, tongue, people, and nation (Rev 5:9), that have been, are, or shall be gathered into one, under Christ, and is the bride (Eph 5:25-32), body, and fullness of Christ (Eph 1:22). The coming of the Spirit on the Day of Pentecost didn't create the people of God but renewed them, fulfilling the promise to Abraham, that the Gentiles would be included in Abraham's seed (Gal 3:14, 29).

God's Visible Witness

God's people are to be salty and bright. As such, in the church, Christ's rule becomes visible as God's people submit to His lordship. This is to be in the totality of life. God's people are to model Christ in everything they think, say and do; reflecting Christ's character. This is the way the world should see Jesus in the church. Yet, however visible the people of God may be to the world at any particular time, it remains invisible, known only to God. Peter Craigie reminds us

---

[4] Grudem, Systematic Theology, 853.

that, "whereas the old covenant had an external form in the nation state, the new covenant would be marked by an inner work of God in man's heart."[5]

This inner work on man's heart, "the answer of a good conscience toward God" (1 Pet 3:21), is made visible in both baptism and in the Lord's Supper. After repentance towards God and faith towards the Lord Jesus Christ, the believer is to publicly proclaim his identity with Christ by water baptism, in the Name of the Father, Son, and Holy Spirit. It is an act of obedience symbolizing the believer's faith in a crucified, buried, and risen Saviour, the believer's death to sin, the burial of the old life, and the resurrection to walk in newness of life in Christ Jesus. It is a testimony to his faith in the final resurrection of the dead. Being a church ordinance, it is prerequisite to the privileges of church membership and to the Lord's Supper.

The Lord's Supper (Communion) is a symbolic act of obedience whereby members of the church, through partaking of the bread and the fruit of the vine, memorialize the death of the Christ and anticipate His second coming. Communion is to be taken frequently and offered to all believers except those who are living in unrepentant rebellion or immorality. The communion elements are symbols of Christ's body and blood and are useful to the exercise of faith in the Person of Jesus Christ as the only means of absolving guilt, shame, and punishment of sin.

These sacraments or ordinances are signs, symbols, and testaments. Signs point, symbols resemble, and testaments testify. Baptism is a sign showing that the

---

[5] Craigie, The Problem of War in the Old Testament, 79.

true believer has been once-for-all incorporated into Christ.[6] That his sins have been forgiven. It shows our union with Christ in His death and our rising together with Him, by regeneration through His resurrection, to walk in newness of life (Rom 6:4; 1 Pet 1:3).

Baptism is a symbol resembling our death to the world and sin's dominion. It corresponds and relates in graphic form to Christ's sufferings and death for our redemption and righteousness. It is the visible gospel. Further, baptism is a testament, in that it bears witness or testifies to the believer's good conscience toward God (1 Pet 3:21) – removal of the guilt of sin through repentance and faith; love for Christ and his subjection to Him (lordship). John Calvin writes, "Baptism is a kind of entrance into the Church, an initiation into the faith, and the Lord's Supper the constant ailment by which Christ spiritually feeds his family of believers."[7] Thus, baptism reflects our once-for-all union with Christ, the Lord's Supper reflects our continuous participation in Him. Christ instituted the Eucharist or Communion so to help Christians grasp the reality of their union with Him in some measure.

The word "communion" κοινωνία koinonia means participation and fellowship. God's people are one body in Christ. Christ indwells His church in the fellowship of the Spirit.[8] Thus, Christians have fellowship with Christ and each other through the Holy Spirit. Perfected fellowship with God is the goal of

---

[6] Biblical signs are physical and temporal phenomenon that have corresponding spiritual and eternal significance. Signs σημεῖον semeon produce faith in those who have ears to hear the gospel (Mt 13:10-17).

[7] Calvin, Institutes of the Christian Religion, Book IV, 19.

[8] Clowney, The Church, 29.

human history.[9] The world should see this fellowship in the church. The Lord's Supper is a sign, symbol, and testament to this truth.

God's Instrument for the Gospel

So far in this fourth mark we've discussed that God has created a covenant community consisting of all believers from every tribe, tongue, people, and nation (Rev 5:9), and that this people are to be a visible witness, reflecting His glory. We now approach God's means for reaching the lost, which is a verbal witness for the saving power of the gospel.

Remember Christ's parable of the strong man (Mt 12:25-30)? Christ penetrates from the heavenly realm into the earthly, defeats Satan by the cross, and begins mankind's restoration with His resurrection. The City of God has come and will be victorious (Isaiah 26)! Christ didn't suggest we proclaim this, He commanded it (Mt 28:18-20). This is the church's message, salvation in Christ alone, by grace alone, through faith alone (Acts 4:12)!

One of the most fundamental truths of the Christian faith is the Incarnation was the coming of God to save us in the heart of our fallen and depraved humanity. God had to send His Son or mankind would be dead, defiled, and damned forever. If Adam's fall injured only himself, as Pelagius reasoned, and if mankind can get their act together and merit God's eternal favor, then why did God send His Son to die for us? This is the prevailing woe of the social gospel, it's merely a help to morally shape culture. But God is renewing humanity

---

[9] Ibid, 173.

in Christ. Mankind is fallen in Adam but raised in Christ (Rom 5:12, 18).

God's instrument for saving the lost is the gospel, and as we saw earlier, the gospel proclamation is like a sword; the very presence of Christ. The testimony of Jesus Christ, that is, a *verbal witness* to His saving power, reveals the truth of mankind's common standing in the sight of God; rebellious sinners that desperately need a Savior (Rom 3:23; 5:12). Christ builds His church through the verbal witness of His saints (Mt 16:17-19).

In our verbal witness, God is making His proclamation to a recalcitrant world. Christ speaks through us when we proclaim the gospel. God's instrument for reclaiming lost sinners is Christ speaking through the church's verbal witness (Is 29:18; Mt 13:3-9; 18-23). The lost come to Christ and fellowship with His people. The church is the house of God, the body of Christ, and the temple of the Holy Spirit. It is therefore in this understanding that we can state with object certainty, "Outside the church there is no salvation," because everyone who is, was, or ever will be saved is included in the number of God's elect (Eph 1:11).[10] *There is only one flock and one Shepherd; God simply has no other saving program* (John 10:16).

The Kingdom has come, the Kingdom is coming, and the Kingdom will come. There is a pronounced tension in all of this which may be felt. George Ladd tells us, the tension between the future and the present is the tension between the Kingdom in complete fulfillment

[10] Election is the gracious purpose of God in the midst of Redemption-History by which God demonstrates His Sovereign acts of saving grace.

and the Kingdom in process of breaking in upon the present order.[11]

The Kingdom of God is a present reality and future hope, forcibly advancing through the agency of the Church. The Kingdom of God includes both His general sovereignty over the universe and His particular kingship over men and women who receive Him as King. Particularly the Kingdom is the realm of salvation into which men enter by trustful, childlike commitment to Jesus Christ. The Church as the Body of Christ, from both the Old and New Testament periods, includes all of the redeemed of all the ages, believers from every tribe, and tongue, and people, and nation. The full consummation of the Kingdom awaits the return of Jesus Christ and the end of this age.

There is a now and not yet tension in all of this, but the Christian life is one of balance so we would do best to let the tension remain. God has established two kingdoms: the church and the state. One is temporary, one is eternal. One is of this world; the other is not of this world. He has given certain authority to each, and has placed certain limitations on each. Why did God establish the state? What is the purpose of the civil government? These are topics of discussion for our next section.

One final question we might ask. What does it mean to be a faithful member of the church? Most churches have constitutions and by-laws which reflect biblical doctrine. Here is an example of what most churches in the Protestant expression consider a faithful church member: "Members are expected to (1) be faithful in all duties of the church; (2) give regularly of their time,

---

[11] Ladd, The Presence of the Future, 7.

talents, and tithes for the support of the church and its causes, and (3) share in the work of its organization." While this seems reasonable, we would do well to remember the words of A.A. Hodge who said, "A church has no right to make anything a condition of membership which Christ has not made a condition of salvation."[12]

One of the goals of attending a local church is Christian maturity, which is fostered through faithful preaching, teaching, fellowship, and the discipline of God's Word. Some Christians demur from attending church; they forsake the assembly to their own hurt (Heb 10:24-25). Other issues that have not been addressed here, such as tithing and missions will be covered in chapter seven.

Being a member of a church involves many responsibilities, but is equally full of many privileges. "We must grasp once again," said Lloyd-Jones, "the idea of church membership as being the membership of the body of Christ and as the biggest honor which can come a man's way in this world."[13]

The author of the Book of Hebrews instructs us not to "forsake assembling together," and the reason is four-fold: First, in order to submit themselves to the teaching of the Holy Scriptures. Second, Christians share a common hope in the gospel and a common fellowship with God in the Spirit. Third, Christians are to regularly worship God and celebrate the Lord's Supper together, and fourth, Christians are to experience the presence and power of God with one another in prayer (Acts 2:42). And besides, for those to

---

[12] Hodge, A Commentary on the Confession of Faith: With Questions for Theological Students and Bible Classes, 21.

[13] Lloyd-Jones, Knowing the Times, 30.

whom he is a Father, the church must also be a mother.[14] "Belonging to the church, as John MacArthur has said, is at the very heart of Christianity." For the church is the pillar and ground of the truth (1 Tim 3:15).

The Lord Jesus Christ baptizes regenerated believers in the Holy Spirit. All the gifts of the Spirit continue to be expressed in the Church today and are subject to the order prescribed in Scripture. As far as spiritual gifts are concerned, the apostle Paul provides no systemization but, emphasizing diversity, he lists them in four groupings of Scripture: Rom 12:6-8; 1 Cor 12:8-10; 1 Cor 12:28-30; and Eph 4: 11. For a local congregation to function correctly, all believers must exercise their gifts of helping (1 Cor 12:28), discerning of spirits (1 Cor 12:10), knowledge (1 Cor 12:8) or whatever gift the Holy Spirit has graced them with. The diversity of gifts is intended by God to promote interdependence – fellowship.

We acknowledge the vital role of the Holy Spirit today, believing local churches should enjoy the presence, power, fruit and gifts of God's Spirit in a way that is beneficial to both believers and unbelievers. And above all, the Spirit empowers us for mission to our neighborhoods and to the nations, in a recovery of New Testament Church Life (Acts 1:4-8).

The Kingdom of God – As the Bible teaches, the Kingdom of God is a present reality and future hope, forcibly advancing through the agency of the Church. The Kingdom of God includes both His general sovereignty over the universe and His particular kingship over men and women who receive Him as King. Particularly the Kingdom is the realm of

[14] Calvin, Institutes of the Christian Religion, 4.1.1, 672.

salvation into which men enter by trustful, childlike commitment to Jesus Christ. The Church as the Body of Christ, from both the Old and New Testament periods, includes all of the redeemed of all the ages, believers from every tribe, and tongue, and people, and nation. The full consummation of the Kingdom awaits the return of Jesus Christ and the end of this age.

Government – Christ rules His church through a plurality of godly men. He qualifies these men by giving them spiritual gifts and prepares them to serve in the local congregation. For the edification of the Church, Christ Jesus has appointed officers not only to preach the Gospel and administer the Sacraments, but also to exercise discipline for the preservation both of truth and duty. It is incumbent upon these officers and upon the whole Church in whose name they act, to censure or cast out the erroneous and scandalous, observing in all cases the rules contained in the Word of God. God gifts and calls men to serve as elders and deacons in the local church which confirms and ordains them to the task of leading and teaching. We believe that God has ordained male leadership in the marriage, family, and church. Biblical church leadership should reflect biblical family leadership.

The Bible is clear in specifying that church officers: teaching Elder, ruling Elder, and Deacon, are to be the husbands of one wife. Therefore, leadership roles in the church are to be filled by godly men (1 Cor 14:35; Tit 2:4). Further, the Bible clearly teaches that while men and women are equal in value (Gen 1:27; Gal 3:28), their roles are different (Ephesians 5:22-33). While both men and women are gifted for service in the church, the church offices of Elder and Deacon are limited to men as qualified by Scripture.

Ordinances – After repentance towards God and faith towards the Lord Jesus Christ, the believer is to publicly proclaim his identity with Christ by water baptism, in the Name of the Father, Son, and Holy Spirit. It is an act of obedience symbolizing the believer's faith in a crucified, buried, and risen Saviour, the believer's death to sin, the burial of the old life, and the resurrection to walk in newness of life in Christ Jesus. It is a testimony to his faith in the final resurrection of the dead.

Being a church ordinance, it is prerequisite to the privileges of church membership and to the Lord's Supper. The Lord's Supper (Communion) is a symbolic act of obedience whereby members of the church, through partaking of the bread and the fruit of the vine, memorialize the death of the Christ and anticipate His second coming. Communion is to be taken frequently and offered to all believers except those who are living in unrepentant rebellion or immorality. The communion elements are symbols of Christ's body and blood and are useful to the exercise of faith in the Person of Jesus Christ as the only means of absolving guilt, shame, and punishment of sin.

Spiritual Gifts – The Lord Jesus Christ baptizes regenerated believers in the Holy Spirit. All the gifts of the Spirit continue to be expressed in the Church today and are subject to the order prescribed in Scripture. For a local congregation to function correctly, all believers must exercise their gifts of helping (1 Cor 12:28), discerning of spirits (1 Cor 12:10), knowledge (1 Cor 12:8) or whatever gift the Holy Spirit has graced them with. The diversity of gifts is intended by God to promote interdependence – fellowship. We acknowledge the vital role of the Holy Spirit today, believing local churches should enjoy the presence, power, fruit and gifts of God's Spirit in a way that is beneficial to both believers and unbelievers. And above all, the Spirit empowers us for mission to our neighborhoods and to the nations, in a recovery of New Testament Church Life (Acts 1:4-8).

Chapter Nine: Doctrine of the Last Things

"In the world you will have tribulation. But take heart; I have overcome the world" (John 16:33).

Eschatology is a part of theology that concerns itself with the last things of history and the ultimate destiny of humanity. Many pastors shy away from preaching and teaching the parts of the Bible that deal with such topics. However, pastors are to preach the whole counsel of God. Besides, what many do not realize is, a person's eschatology drives their soteriology. In other words, our view of the end times effects in large measure our view of salvation.

The word "eschatology" comes from two Greek words *eskhatos* ἔσχατος which means "last" and *logia* λογία meaning to "study." Eschatology covers a broad spectrum of events. In this chapter, our goal is to trace out four essential areas of eschatology: (1) the Inaugurated End Times, (2) the Intermediate State, (3) the Second Coming of Christ, and (4) the Final Judgment and the Eternal State.

At the close of John's Revelation, the Lord Jesus says, "I make all things new" (Rev 21:5). Eschatology may be therefore understood as the manner in which the Christ is doing precisely that. While there are undeniable difficulties in the Book of Revelation, which is one of the reasons why the church at large leaves it alone, when it comes to a study of the end times, it's the *sine qua non* of Books for essentially three reasons: First, God gave the Church the Book of Revelation to show us reality and how God's going to act to bring about the end He has decreed (Rev 5). Second, God gave us the Book of Revelation to encourage His Church that regardless of what it looks like, Jesus is the King of kings (Rev 1:5). And third, God gave us the Book of Revelation so that His suffering, persecuted Church might persevere in faith (Rev 14:12).

Inaugurated End Times – The Book of Revelation is a vision not a video tape of the future. This is a needful distinction because much in the Revelation is symbolic. Instead of a detailed history of the future, Revelation is a representation of the past, present and future of world history through signs, symbols, images and visions. Revelation 1:19 undergirds this fact when the risen Christ commands John: "Write therefore the things that you *have seen, those that are* and *those that are to take place after this*."

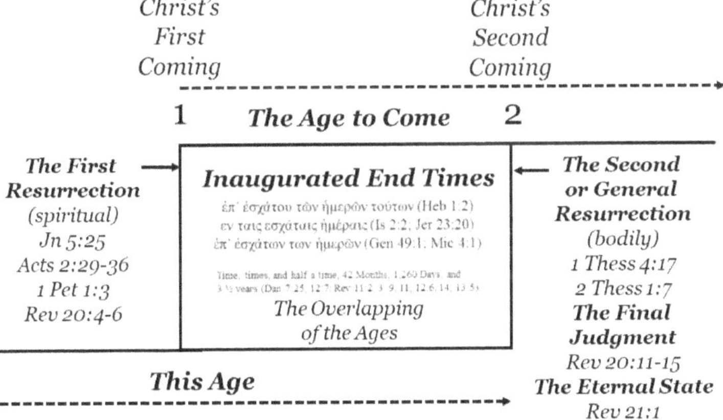

Figure 9-1. Inaugurated End Times.

The point being here is, we are already living in the end times or last days. As the author of the Book of Hebrews states emphatically, "God, who at various times and in various ways spoke in time past to the fathers by the prophets, has in these last days spoken to us by His Son" (Heb 1:1-2; cf. 1 Pet 4:7). The term we use to describe living in between Christ's first and second advents is "inaugurated end times." This is the belief that the end times were inaugurated or began in the life, death and resurrection of Jesus, and that we are currently living in the overlapping of this age and the age to come. The term "inaugurated end times" therefore characterizes the "already" and "not yet" aspects to the Kingdom of God.

The Book of Revelation is written to seven churches in the First Century Roman Province of Asia (Modern Turkey), who are facing a growing opposition to Christianity by way of a pagan culture and a Roman government in which many were paying with their lives. Writing from the Isle of Patmos, John identifies himself with fellow Christians as "your brother and fellow partaker" in the tribulation and kingdom and patient endurance of Jesus Christ (Rev 1:9). There is a world of theology in this one verse. This means the church, as brothers and fellow partakers of Christ's kingdom, must continue to endure tribulation, while faithfully testifying the gospel, until all of God's people are saved and then the end will come (Mt 24:14; Jn 16:33; Rom 11:26).

Christ gave His church teaching on tribulation because His intent was for the church to not only survive all tribulation, including the "Great Tribulation," but to conquer through it. The phrase "Great Tribulation" is a technical term referring to the end time trial which has already been set in motion by Christ's first coming and will culminate with His second coming (Acts 14:22; 1 Cor 11:25; Rev 7:14).

The Intermediate State – The Bible teaches us that when we die, we go to one of two places, heaven or hell. Beside these two places, for souls separated from their bodies, the Scripture acknowledges none. At death, the souls of the redeemed are made perfect in holiness and immediately enter into the presence of Christ, enjoying conscious fellowship with Him, there to wait the resurrection of the body.

The intermediate state is a person's "intermediate" existence between death and the resurrection. As the Bible teaches, the state of unbelievers after death is a fixed state which corresponds to the final judgment, as determined by the things that are done in the flesh (Mt 10:32, 33; 25:34–46; Lk 12:47, 48; Gal. 6:7; 2 Thess 1:8; Heb. 9:27). As for believers, the Bible represents them as enjoying a conscious life in communion with God and with Jesus Christ immediately after death (Lk 16:19–31; Acts 7:59; 2 Cor 5:8; Phil 1:23; Rev. 6:9; 7:9; 20:4).

The Second Coming – According to His promise, Jesus Christ will return bodily, visibly, and personally in glory to the earth; the dead will be raised; and Christ will judge all men in righteousness. According to 1 Thessalonians 4:13-5:1, the Day of the Lord is to be consummated by the coming of the Lord Jesus Christ again. Those who are found alive shall not die, but be changed: and all the dead shall be raised up, with the same bodies, although with different qualities, which shall be united again to their souls forever. The bodies of the unjust shall, by the power of Christ, be raised to dishonor: the bodies of the just, by His Spirit, unto honor; and be made conformable to His own glorious body.

The Final Judgment – On the Great Day of judgment (the Day of the Lord), the unrighteous will be consigned to Hell, the place of everlasting punishment, while the righteous in their resurrected and glorified bodies will receive their reward and will dwell forever in Heaven with the Lord. The bodies of men, after death, return to dust, and see corruption: but their souls, which neither die nor sleep, having an immortal subsistence, immediately return to God who gave them: the souls of the righteous, being then made perfect in holiness, are received into the highest heavens, where they behold the face of God, in light and glory, waiting for the full redemption of their bodies. And the souls of the wicked are cast into hell, where they remain in torments and utter darkness, reserved to the judgment of the great day.

Regarding the view of the millennium, there are essentially three main approaches or schools: premillennial, amillennial and postmillennial. Amillennial and Postmillennial views understand the millennium of Revelation 20:1-6 to be the interadvent period; with a further differentiation being, in the Amillennial position Christ's reign began with His incarnation, ministry, crucifixion, and intercession, etc. while Postmillennials, differing about the timing of the binding of Satan, see the binding as some future event, an event that will eventually lead to a global Christian world.

Let it be said, however, that many Postmills place the binding at the first advent, and thus have little difference with many Amills. Over against these schools of eschatology is premillennialism, which itself includes two approaches: the Historic Premillennial and Dispensational Premillennial viewpoints. Both of these Premill positions understand the millennium to begin after Christ's second advent. Historic Premillennialism differs from Dispensational Premillennialism in their view of the saving program of God: Dispensational Premills hold that there are two distinct peoples of God – Israel and the church, and that the 1000-year reign of Christ on earth is with Israel, not the church while Historic Premills do not.

Tribulation-Kingdom-Endurance

The Book of Revelation is full of sets of seven. The first of the Seven Beatitudes in Revelation is found in Rev 1:3, "Blessed is he who reads and those who hear the words of this prophecy, and keep those things which are written in it; for the time is near." There are three participles in this verse, that is, action verbs ending in "ing," words like "reading," "hearing," and "observing." In the original Greek this reads, blessed are those who are reading and hearing the words of this prophecy and observing the things that are written in it. In other words, we are blessed if we read and hear the Book of Revelation and do what Christ commands us in it. Commands like, "keep your first love," "endure," "stop compromising," etc.

Looking again at these eschatological triad, tribulation refers to persecution, affliction, distress which comes on account of the gospel witness. Kingdom is the exercise of Christ's rule in the present and future kingdom of Christ, and patient endurance is remaining faithful to Christ despite tribulation.

Tribulation – Tribulation is not only part and parcel of the saints anticipated earthly sojourn, it also serves to wield and temper Christ's corporate body into an effective instrument for emancipating the lost (Jn 16:33). Thus, tribulations come upon Christ by way of His followers (Jn 16:33; Col 1:24; 2 Tim 3:12). As the world hates and persecutes the church, it is doing so to Christ (Acts 9:4-5; cf. Is 63:9). Christ gave the church the Book of Revelation because tribulation will end only with His second advent (2 Thess 1:6-7; Rev 12:13-17).[1]

As the Scriptures also teach, God has a redemptive purpose for tribulation (2 Cor 1:6). Persecution from an unbelieving world is meant for evil, but God ordains it for His glory and the good of His church (Gen 50:19-20; Rom 8:28). What's more, God preserves believers safely in the hands of Christ (Jn 10:28-29). According to Christ's promise, "In the world you will have tribulation; but be of good cheer, I have overcome the world" (Jn 16:33).

Kingdom – Christians, says our Lord Jesus, are sons of the kingdom, and as such are to be primarily concerned with the coming and further expansion of that kingdom (Mt 6:9-13, 24-33). Christ Jesus, by conquering the powers of darkness in His incarnation, obedience, crucifixion, resurrection, and ascension is our present reigning King (Rom 1:4; Col 1:13-18); and the present "ruler over the kings of the earth" (Rev 1:5).

Believers are presently brought into Christ's kingdom by faith to be held in the divine grasp and endure to the end (Jn 5:25; 10:28). Believers now have a share in Christ's kingdom by obedient lives and bearing witness to His saving power (Rev 1:9; 12:11). Christ's Kingdom has come, and is coming, and will

---

[1] Greg K. Beale, *New Testament Biblical Theology: The Unfolding of the Old Testament in the New* (Grand Rapids, MI: Baker, 2011), 218.

come. George E. Ladd has well observed, "The age of fulfillment is not only near; it is actually present. Nevertheless, the time of apocalyptic consummation remains in the future." This is the "now" and the "not yet" of the Kingdom of God. There is a felt tension in all of this as Greg Beale informs us,

> John and his community are people who even now reign together in Jesus' kingdom. The exercise of rule in this kingdom begins and continues only as one faithfully endures tribulation. This is a formula for kingship: faithful endurance through tribulation is the means by which one reigns in the present with Jesus. Their endurance is part of the process of "conquering."[2]

In other words, the Kingdom of God is both a present reality and a future hope.

Those who willingly surrender to Christ now, experience the saving power of His cross, a peace of conscience and spiritually enter His Kingdom (Mt 4:17; 11:28-30); those who reject Him experience a judicial hardening for their sins, an ever-increasing confused, agitated conscience until they face an angry God in judgment where they will be justly condemned for their sins, and will be punished with the everlasting torments of hell (Mt 22:13; 25:30).

Endurance – Endurance is staying power which can only be acquired through testing, and suffering. For example, the apostle Paul tells us in Rom 5:3-4, "We also glory in tribulations, knowing that tribulation produces perseverance; and perseverance, character;

---

[2] Greg K. Beale, *The Book of Revelation: A Commentary on the Greek Text* (Grand Rapids, MI: Baker, 1999), 201.

and character, hope." What character is the apostle Paul talking about? The very character of Christ, Who Himself is forming Himself within us. This doesn't mean, of course, that we have only a hope of future joys, we can be full of joy here and now even in our trials and troubles.

Taken in the right spirit these very things will give us patient endurance; this in turn will develop a mature character. A character of this sort produces a steady hope, a hope that will never disappoint us because if we are born again, already we have some experience of the love of God flooding through our hearts by the Holy Spirit given to us. Sufferings temper Christians and is part of God's discipline.

Together, Christians are brothers and fellow partakers in the tribulation and kingdom and patient endurance of Jesus Christ (Rev 1:9). As we minister in Christ's kingdom, we are compelled by the love of Christ to witness to His saving power, which is assured the world's hatred and brings tribulation, through which we are enabled to endure to the end by His presence. The kingdom is present in Jesus. And God is making His appeal to the world through His church to be reconciled to Him (2 Cor 5:20-21).

Faith lays hold of the promises of God in Christ and breaks forth into action – telling people about the saving power of Jesus Christ. But this work of faith brings with it the world's hatred (Gen 3:15). And so, tribulation ensues, ushering in its train a progressive pressure and maddening violence which seeks to eradicate the offending witness that brought the threat of destruction – repent and believe the gospel or suffer the fires of hell forever (Mt 3:7-12). The truths of the gospel of the kingdom are hidden by a judicial act of

God, from those who, in their own estimation, are the wise and prudent. They cannot see the light of the gospel because they trust their own dim light, and will not accept the light of God. The gospel enlightens some but blinds others (Jn 9:39-41). In spite of it all, love labors long, guiding the work of faith, enabling believers, as mediating priests, to be self-squanders in Christ service, seeking the recovery of the lost (2 Cor 5:14, 20). Christ enlarges our hearts to include others so that we might by all means save some (1 Cor 9:22). The continuing loyalty to Christ despite persecution serves to define our character and produces endurance by which we may hope large in our inheritance – God Himself, at our coming resurrection.

All of this is brought together by Jesus in His Olivet Discourse (Mt 24). When answering the disciples' questions regarding: (1) when will be the destruction of the temple? (2) when will be the sign of His coming? And (3) when will be the consummation of the age? Jesus told them some things relating to the destruction of Jerusalem, some things about His second coming, and some things which would immediately precede the end of the world.

It would seem Jesus makes a point to answer the last two questions before the first. Namely, there will be a delay characterized by persecution and tribulation for His followers before His return (Mt 24:4-14). As for the first question, Jesus describes in vivid detail how Jerusalem will undergo, in the near future, a violent destruction, which will stand as a type signifying the manner in which a world-full of obstinate rebels shall in the end likewise perish (Mt 24:15-28).

As to the other two questions, Jesus describes for His disciples the inter-advent period in Matthew 24:4-14.

Jesus characterizes the period of time between His first and second comings as a time of false prophets, wars, famines, pestilences, and earthquakes. And in Mt 24:9-14 He says,

> 9 "Then they will deliver you up to tribulation and kill you, and you will be hated by all nations for My name's sake. 10 And then many will be offended, will betray one another, and will hate one another. 11 Then many false prophets will rise up and deceive many. 12 And because lawlessness will abound, the love of many will grow cold. 13 But he who endures to the end shall be saved. 14 And this gospel of the kingdom will be preached in all the world as a witness to all the nations, and then the end will come (emphasis added).

These words of Jesus give us the express purpose of preaching – a witness to all nations. The goal of preaching the "gospel of the kingdom" is for "every tribe and tongue and people and nation" to hear the glorious saving power of Christ's cross. So that they might by faith surrender to King Jesus and love and obey Him.

I find in these words of Jesus a command, a cost, and confidence which is ultimately buttressed with the Great Commission (Mt 28:18-20). "This gospel of the kingdom will be preached in all the world as a witness to all the nations," is a command, not a suggestion (Mt 24:14). "They will deliver you up to tribulation and kill you, and you will be hated by all nations for My name's sake," is the cost for the completion of the Great Commission (Mt 24:9). And "He who endures to the end shall be saved," is the confidence which a perfect atonement secures (Mt 24:13). As Christians, we are enabled to do this because we have been crucified with Christ, Who now dwells in our hearts by faith with which He roots and grounds Himself to us in love, which is the power that compels us to minister in His kingdom, as we proclaim the gospel; mankind's only hope for forgiveness and salvation and the resurrection (Gal 2:20).

Christians are brothers and fellow partakers in the tribulation and kingdom and patient endurance of Jesus Christ (Rev 1:9). We are enabled to persevere in faith through a period of time (between Christ's First and Second Advents) which is characterized by persecution and tribulation for His followers (Mt 24:4-14, cf. Heb 7:25). During this period, believers serve God as a kingdom of ministering-witnessing priests, who proclaim the saving truths of the gospel of the kingdom. D.A. Carson cogently writes, "If all of God's sovereignty is even now mediated through Jesus, Jesus is reigning – but He is doing so in the teeth of sustained opposition: He reigns until He has put all enemies under His feet, and utterly destroyed the last enemy, death itself" (1 Cor 15:25).

As has been said, the Kingdom has come, the Kingdom is coming, and the Kingdom will come. The Baptist Faith and Message succinctly puts it,

> The Kingdom of God includes both His general sovereignty over the universe and His particular Kingship over men who willfully acknowledge Him as King. Particularly the Kingdom is the realm of salvation into which men enter by trustful, childlike commitment to Jesus Christ. Christians ought to pray and labor that the Kingdom may come and God's will be done on earth. The full consummation

> of the Kingdom awaits the return of Jesus Christ and the end of this age.

The point is this: Christians enter Christ's kingdom now spiritually, and are called to remain faithful to Christ and engage their culture, seeking to win the lost.

The church, God's instrument of evangelism, is to go out, charged with this command: "And this gospel of the kingdom will be preached in all the world as a witness to all the nations, and then the end will come" (Mt 24:14). This is both the manner in which the full number of God's people will be brought in, and the event that will usher in the climactic return of the King.

The gospel is God's restoration program for mankind, who are fallen in Adam's physical and spiritual death, but by grace through faith are raised in Christ's resurrection, first spiritually, then physically (Jn 5:25-29; 1 Pet 1:3; 2 Pet 3:10).

In summary, Christ will return at the end of the world for the purpose of introducing the future age, the eternal state of things, and He will do this by inaugurating and completing two mighty events, namely, the resurrection of the dead and the final judgment (Mt 13:49, 50; 16:27; 24:3; 25:14–30; Lk 9:26; 19:15, 26, 27; Jn 5:25–29; Acts 17:31; Rom 2:3–16; 1 Cor 4:5; 15:23; 2 Cor. 5:10; Phil. 3:20, 21; 1 Thess 4:13–17; 2 Thess 1:7–10; 2:7, 8; 2 Tim 4:1, 8; 2 Pet 3:10–13; Jude 14, 15; Rev 20:11–15; 22:12).

Part Three: Seven Core Duties

A pastor is called to preach the Word, teach the truth to God's people, lead God's people in worship, tend the flock as a caring shepherd, and mobilize the church for Christian witness and service.[1] To that end, here in part three, the aim will be to outline what constitutes the seven core duties of a pastor: Worship, leadership, disciple-making, evangelism, preaching and teaching, counseling, watching and warning.

---

[1] R. Albert Mohler Jr., quoted in *On Being a Pastor* (Chicago, IL: Moody, 2004), 9.

Chapter Ten: Worship

"You cannot find excellent corporate worship until you stop trying to find excellent corporate worship and pursue God himself." – D.A. Carson

The year is 67 AD. The Apostle Paul is a prisoner in Rome. He expects that any day he will be taken before the Emperor Nero and be executed. He has faced this sort of thing before when he was in Rome under house. But after a couple of years, in about 62 AD, he was released and returns to his apostolic work, travelling to Crete and to Asia Minor, preaching the gospel. But now he has been arrested again and is taken back to Rome. Things now go from bad to worse. Many of his ministry colleagues have disserted him (2 Tim 1:15). Winter is also coming on and Paul writes his second letter to his spiritual son – Timothy.

Timothy is in the city of Ephesus, which at that time was one of the greatest cities in the ancient world. At around 250,000 inhabitants, Ephesus was known as the "Gateway of Asia," and was the capital and most prominent of all the cities in the Roman province of Asia Minor. Sprawling out in a great valley, the city was nestled between two mountain ranges. In ancient times, it had a harbor that connected it to the Aegean Sea.[1] Famously, the most prominent part of Ephesus was the temple of Artemis, which was one of the seven wonders of the ancient world. Because of this, the city's economy was almost entirely devoted to idolatry and

[1] Colin F. Hemer, *The Letters to the Seven Churches of Asia in Their Local Setting* (Grand Rapids: Eerdmans, 1986), 36.

sexual immorality. Paul spent a few years working at Ephesus and revisited the city several times during his missionary travels. During his second trip, he gifted the church there with Aquila and Priscilla (Acts 18:18-21). Then, on his third missionary journey, Paul spent about three years there, preaching and teaching the whole council of God (Acts 20:27). From this bestowment of apostolic attention and grace, the city of Ephesus was known to have a keen eye for doctrine (Rev 2:2). And before Paul departed the city after some three and a half years of ministry, he set in his young ministry friend Timothy as pastor.

Back in Rome, Paul doesn't know how long he has to live. Only his old travelling companion Luke is with him. Paul doesn't know if he will see Timothy again, so he doesn't just tell him to come quickly. Instead, Paul writes to him the things he will need to know after Paul dies. And what Paul writes to Timothy is the apostle's final instructions to a young pastor who is facing all the trials and complexities of Christian ministry. This moving letter, is Paul's last. In it, the apostle encapsulates the distilled instructions of a seasoned pastor to Timothy, as well as all of God's men. Paul wants Timothy to know that after he is gone, Timothy, along with those he appoints, must carry on the work of preaching the gospel of Jesus Christ. Paul wants Timothy, and all of us, to take on this mantle. Paul is passing the torch.

As the first fundamental doctrine, theology begins with knowing God. Believers come to know God because He first reveals Himself to us (Rom 1:20), and communicates His love to us (1 Jn 4:19).

God created man to worship Him. Worshipping God is therefore to be our chief joy and highest aim in this life and in the next. The English word "worship" comes from the Anglo-Saxon word *weorthscipe*, which relates to value and worthiness. And so, in the true sense of this word, true worship is valuing God above all things. Worth-ship is valuing God for His matchless worth.

True worship is given when we know God and our hearts are right with Him. Psalm 96:5 tells us that all the gods of the peoples are worthless idols (in the LXX demons). There is only one true God, the rest are demons, who call for the worship of mankind, seeking to usurp the worship due God alone (Gal 4:8). The reason false gods (demons) have this enslaving power is because by demonic force they gain mastery over their worshippers.

The Bible reveals the covenant making and covenant keeping God. Beginning with Genesis we may trace out the progress of redemption as God takes a people for His very own (Lev 26:11). In the Exodus, God's purpose was to bring a people out of Egypt to serve Him, literally to worship Him as priests (Ex 4:23; cf. Rom 12:1). As the descendants of Abraham, Israel was in bondage both physically and spiritually. The gods of Egypt held real spiritual power over the minds and hearts of the Egyptians, as well as the Israelites. God called and gifted His servant Moses to lead His people out of Egypt. With an outstretch arm, God brought them out of the house bondage. The Exodus was therefore judgment to release captives. It was the reconstitution of the Israelites, making them a nation. God's purpose in the Exodus was to create a holy nation, a kingdom of priests (Ex 19:4-6).

Being made a nation, Israel was to carry out God's purposes. Her mission was to live in obedience to God in the land God would give her so that the nations would be drawn to her light. The mission of Israel was to be blessed to be a blessing. This was in fact what God promised Abraham when He called him out of his country and family saying: "I will bless those who bless you, and I will curse him who curses you; and in you all the families of the earth shall be blessed" (Gen 12:3).

Bringing His people out of Egypt, God gave them His royal law which preeminently prescribed how God was to receive worship. Additionally, the law not only taught the people God's concerns for holiness, it also prefigured through types and shadows the Redeemer of God's people. God also gave the people the tabernacle which was itself a symbol of His presence and the meeting place between God and man.

God's servant Moses as spokesman, lawgiver, and mediator taught the people the need to pay careful attention to God's revelation, to be holy, separate from the nations, that living in the Land of Promise was conditioned on covenant loyalty. God then planted His people in the Promised Land, itself a type of the heavenly inheritance. Having brought them out of Egypt, God considered Himself a Shepherd and Israel was the sheep of His pasture.

Following the turbulent time of the Judges, "the people asked for a king; so God gave them Saul" (Acts 13:22). And after God removed him, He gave the people David and through him the kingdom was established. As God's servant, David shepherded the people of God, defeated their enemies, and from his seed, "according to the promise, God raised up for Israel a Savior – Jesus" (Acts 13:23). David's son Solomon then built the temple of God and Israel enjoyed the covenant blessings of God as she lived in obedience. Solomon's reign consolidated David's aspirations for peace, and, above all, the presence of God in the temple.[1] The Lord reminded Solomon, that as king, the blessings of the covenant community of Israel depended on his continued faithfulness (1 Kings 6:12-13).

While Israel enjoyed many blessings under Solomon, he nevertheless fell into idolatry and did not fully follow the Lord as his father had. What follows is the story of the divided kingdoms of Israel and Judah. The unrighteousness of the Northern kingdom (Israel), led to God's judgment and their subsequent destruction despite the prophetic pronouncements. While the Southern kingdom (Judah) was not itself ideal, it nonetheless had more "good" kings than Israel had.

Then, some 700 years before Christ, God summoned His servant Isaiah to prophesy. Through Isaiah, God's indicts Judah for her idolatry, immorality and injustice. As Walt Kaiser observes, "God's call to service and His election as instruments of His grace brought with it the obligation and responsibility to be a blessing to all the families of the earth."[2] However, the people's worship has become idolatrous, as touching morality, they parade their sin like Sodom and instead of justice and righteousness there is bloodshed (Is 5:7). For this infidelity, God pronounces the covenant curse. What will transpire as recompense is exile from the land.

---

[1] Willem Van Gemeren, *The Progress of Redemption* (Grand Rapids, MI: Zondervan, 1988), 220.

[2] Walter C. Kaiser Jr., *Mission in the Old Testament: Israel As a Light to the Nations* (Grand Rapids, MI: Baker, 2000), 9.

The captivity will serve to reorder the priorities of God's people. But there's hope. God announces the restored blessings of the covenant that will come about by way of the work of His Servant. As God's Elect Servant, His mission is to take up the failed mission of Israel (Is 42:18-19), to settle a true judgment that Yahweh alone is to be worshipped, to reveal God's Law, establish God's just order (the Kingdom), and restore God's covenant people (Is 49:5-7).

In the Book of Isaiah, the whole nation of Israel is referred at least nine times to as the Lord's "servant." In the other occurrences, "the servant refers to a righteous individual within the nation who serves the nation." Moreover, the Servant of the Lord replaces Israel as the "active dispenser of the word of God to the nations and to the ends of the earth."[3] The Servant is identified in Four Songs (Is 42:1-4; 49:1-6; 50:4-9; 52:13-53:12). The Servant is also the Messiah, the Davidic King.

It is through this Servant that God's righteous purpose will finally be accomplished. It is important to note that the servant of the Lord is a corporate term. In other words, servant of the Lord embodies at one and the same time a reference to the One, as the representative of the whole, as well as the whole group that belongs to that single whole. The Servant of the Lord may be therefore understood as a Corporate Person (1 Cor 12).

The Mission of the Suffering Servant is to: Bring justice to the nations (42:1); be a covenant for the people and a light for the Gentiles (42:6); restore the nation of Israel (49:5-6); to be a guilt offering (53:10)

---

[3] Ibid., 56.

and thereby provide reconciliation and redemption (53:5-6). The resulting work of the Suffering Servant is that many servants are raised up (Is 54).

Israel having failed, the task of being light to the Gentiles is assigned to the Servant, who will take the hand of the remnant of Israel, and in the restoration of the covenant and true worship, will guide them in the work of witnessing, bringing about God's just order.

Jesus Restored True Worship

God alone is to be worshipped. With that as a settled truth, there are two major principles that pertain to the worship of God: First, we are to worship God in the right way. And second, we are to worship Him in the right attitude. The Lord Jesus teaches us these two principles in John chapter four when He meets a Samaritan woman at Jacob's well.

The woman opens a discussion on worship. In her understanding, worship deals only in external realities. Therefore, she says: "Our fathers worshiped on this mountain (Mt. Gerizim), and you Jews say that in Jerusalem is the place where one ought to worship" (Jn 4:20). Jesus said to her:

> Woman, believe Me, the hour is coming when you will neither on this mountain, nor in Jerusalem, worship the Father. You worship what you do not know; we know what we worship, for salvation is of the Jews. But the hour is coming, and now is, when the true worshipers will worship the Father in spirit and truth; for the Father is seeking such to worship Him. God is Spirit, and those who worship Him must worship in spirit and truth (Jn 4:21-24).

True worship, says Jesus, is in "spirit" and in "truth." The first principle is we are to worship God in the right way. And as Jesus teaches us, the central issue is: Not where but Who. In other words, it's not about a place but a Person. Crucial to this entire discussion is what Jesus says before John 4:21. Beginning in John 4:10, Jesus says He is the "gift of God," and that through Him comes "living water." These words of Jesus echo Isaiah 12 where it is said that those who live in Zion, that is, those who have experienced salvation, "with joy" draw water from the "wells of salvation" (Is 12:3). Likewise, in Ezekiel 47, living water flows out of the true temple. And wherever the river goes, there is life and healing (Ezek 47:7-12).

The New Testament declares that the Church is the true temple of God (1 Cor 3:9, 16) that is founded on Jesus Christ, the chief cornerstone (Eph 2:20; cf. Jn 2:19). The Church is the dwelling place of God in the Spirit (Eph 2:22; cf. 1 Pet 2:5). Therefore, what Jesus is saying in John 4:21-24 is: the place of true worship has now been universalized to any place where the Spirit resides in believers, that is, those who are born of the Spirit (Jn 3:5).

Second, we are to worship the Father in the right attitude. Genuine worship therefore flows from our hearts, and is therefore not an external activity. Moreover, the worship that flows truly from our hearts is because we know what Jesus has accomplished for us. Regarding this Kent Hughes rightly observes, "Worshipping in truth means that we come informed by the objective revelation of God's Word."[4] In other

---

[4] Kent Hughes, *Disciplines of a Godly Man* (Wheaton, IL: Crossway, 2001), 114.

words, we cannot give ourselves to a God we don't known (Acts 17:23). Worship is true when it flows out of a heart made pure by God's grace, in knowledge of the redemptive work of Jesus on the cross, whereby we are justified by His death and saved by His life (Rom 4:25). How can those who have experienced His covenant blessings not praise His name?[5]

All of our worship points to the perfect sacrifice of Jesus at Calvary, which forever removed the necessity of the sacrificial system. Christ's sacrifice of Himself on the cross confirmed that the sacrificial system of the Old Testament was not the final solution, but that through the sacrifice of Jesus we would be accepted. Worshipping God in this knowledge is the kind of worship God seeks (Jn 4:23).

The word worship appears ten times in John chapter four. In the Greek the word is προσκυνέω *proskuneo* (the Hebrew equivalent is *shacah*). Προσκυνέω *proskuneo* means to bend down, to kiss, or to prostrate oneself. This is the same word that is used when the Magi from the East came to see the baby Jesus, the text says they bowed down and worshiped Him (Mt 2:11).[6]

Therefore, in light of what the New Testament teaches about Jesus, we understand "worship the Father in spirit" to mean the following: True worship is the worship of God the Father through the Lord Jesus Christ by the Holy Spirit. Likewise, as D. A. Carson rightly observes, true worship is worship that is "God-centered, made possible by the gift of the Holy Spirit,

---

[5] Richard Belcher, *The Messiah and the Psalms*, 47.

[6] See also Matthew 4:10; 8:2; 9:18; 14:33; 15:25; 28:9, 17.

and in personal knowledge of and conformity to God's Word made flesh," Jesus Christ – God incarnate.[7]

Therefore, worship that is in spirit and in truth is not about a place, it's about a Person. Jesus is the place where worshippers meet God. As High Priest, Jesus is the One mediating for us in the presence of the Father (Heb 9:11-28). Jesus is greater than any temple made with human hands (Mt 12:6). True worship occurs when a person who has been saved by the Son meets with the Father through the Holy Spirit. And what occurs in that meeting, in the life of the one who is praising God is, that person finds grace, peace, the love of God, and joy unspeakable.

All Life is Worship

There is an age-old "inhouse" debate as to what constitutes the Church's chief task. Some say evangelism, some discipleship and others worship. I believe worship is the supreme task of the church. For consider, as the Church fulfills its role as a kingdom of mediating priests, people are saved, become worshippers of God and are discipled. Worship is therefore the preeminent function of the church. The church is called to worship God and evangelize the world. Worship is the church's Godward activity while evangelism its man-ward activity.

When we come to Paul's epistles, we further learn that all of life is spiritual worship, and every believer is a priest who is to offer himself as a sacrifice "holy and acceptable to God," according to the pattern laid down

[7] D. A. Carson, *The Gospel According to John* (Grand Rapids, MI: Eerdmans, 1991), 225.

by Christ (Rom 12:2; Rev 1:6). The priesthood of believers is the Christian doctrine that states that all believers have direct access to God through the mediation of Jesus Christ (1 Tim 2:5-6). Affirming this doesn't negate the necessity of the ordained ministry. God saves us and calls us into one fellowship and further appoints some of His saints to serve Him in the ordained ministry, equipping them with gifts commensurate to the task.

Back in Rome, the Apostle Paul doesn't know how long he has to live. His concern is to give Timothy and a line of pastors the instructions we need to serve God's people as under shepherds. As we read Paul's opening paragraph in the Letter of Second Timothy, we find the whole first paragraph saturated with the language of worship.

The praise and thanks of the lips is called a sacrifice to God (Heb 13:15). In 2 Timothy 1:3 Paul declares, "I thank God, whom I ***serve*** with a pure conscience, as my forefathers did." The word "serve" in the Greek is *latreon* λατρείαν which means "priestly service." This is worship that is rendered from the whole man, by the Spirit (in spirit and in truth). Paul calls his own ministry a priestly service of worship, and calls those he has won for Christ an "acceptable offering" to God (Rom 15:16; cf. Phil 2:17). He even calls the money that the churches send him "a fragrant aroma and acceptable sacrifice to God" (Phil 4:18). Paul's own approaching death for Christ he calls a "drink offering to God" (2 Tim 4:6).

As a body of mediating priests, Paul teaches the people of God are the New Testament "temple" where spiritual sacrifices are offered and where God dwells by his Spirit. In 2 Corinthians 6:16, Paul declares: "We are the temple of the living God; just as God said, 'I will dwell in them and walk among them; and I will be their God, and they shall be My people.'"

Paul's desire is for Timothy and us to preach and teach such things, for worship is not just on Sunday, its is to be every day and done in every place where the Spirit resides in believers. What Paul teaches Timothy in a pastor is called lead God's people in worship, demonstrating what a life of sacrifice for Christ looks like. It is common knowledge that various doctrinal, moral and social problems in the Church at Corinth prompted Paul's attention. It light of this, it is a pastor's chief task to insure his congregation's worship does not succumb to the problems that plagued Corinth.

As God's men, we must ensure that our example doesn't contradict our doctrine. All life is worship, and the doctrines we preach must first have worked their power in our own lives. As the puritan pastor John Owen once put it, "If it doesn't dwell with power in us, it will not pass with power from us." We must therefore ensure we don't live in the very sins we preach against lest when we've preached to others, we should become disqualified (1 Cor 9:27). Richard Baxter put it this way, "If we would be skillful in governing others, we must learn first to command ourselves." We must watch our lives and doctrine closely. Persevering in them, because if we do, we will save both ourselves and our hearers (1 Tim 4:16).

We are to preach that worshiping God is the duty of every human being. Worship is proclaiming the worth of God. Worshipping God is a commandment (Ex 20:2-3; Mk 4:10). Our worship of God is not a meritorious work. In our local churches we worship through reading God's Word, singing God's Word, preaching

God's Word, and seeing God's Word in the Sacraments. And the God who is worshipped in Christian adoration is the God revealed in Jesus Christ His Son.

We have called worship a duty because it's a command (Mk 4:10). However, we should not think of duty as something that rigid and dry. Rather, real worship is a delight. As pastors, we have been called to lead God's people in worship. True worship comes from a heart that is made pure by the holy love of God. In this sense, our duty to worship the Lord is a delight. The chief end of man is to glorify God by enjoying him forever. That is worship.

Chapter Eleven: Leadership

"Remember those who rule over you, who have spoken the word of God to you, whose faith follow, considering the outcome of their conduct." – Hebrews 13:7

Leadership is hard to measure, and difficult to describe, yet, we know good leadership when we see it. Moreover, when it is absent, there is often a vacuum of purpose and direction. Without godly leadership, families are destroyed and churches can wander into doctrinal error and heresy.

The word used for leadership in the Greek is προΐστημι proistemi and means "to be over," "to superintend," "preside over," "rule over, and direct" (1 Thess 5:12). By this we understand how Christian leaders keep the church focused on its mission, keep the gospel of Jesus Christ central and equip the saints for works of service (Eph 4:12).

What follows is a discussion regarding the character and qualifications that are required of spiritual leaders in the church, specifically those who serve in the ordained offices of pastor, elder, and deacon.

Part of God's endowment of gifts to His church is leadership (Rom 12:8). In the early church, the apostles would proclaim the gospel, gather God's people together, thereby establishing the church in every city to which they were sent. Then they would ordain pastors or elders from among the local believers to carry on the work of shepherding the people (Acts 14:21-23; Tit 1:5). Regarding this, John MacArthur observes, "The twelve apostles led the early church until it spread out and elders and deacons were trained to lead and serve in other congregations. Because everyone was a new convert in the early church, God left the Twelve with the Jerusalem church for at least seven years."[1]

Regarding leadership in the church, the Apostle Paul tells us "If a man desires the position of a bishop (elder), he desires a good work. The terms elder, pastor-teacher, and over-seer (translated bishop or presbyter) refer to the same office. These terms are used to describe various aspects of the same ministry.[2]

God gifts and calls men to serve as pastors in the local church which confirms and ordains them to the task of leading and teaching. The Bible furnishes no provision for women to serve as pastors. The Bible says, "Let a woman learn in silence with all submission. And I do not permit a woman to teach or to have authority over a man, but to be in silence" (1 Tim 2:11-12; cf. 1 Cor 14:34-38). The reasons for this are not because Paul was prejudiced against women, as many claim, or because the Bible was written in a first century cultural context, rather the reasons are rooted in the creation order: "For Adam was formed first, then Eve" (1 Tim 2:13).[3]

Christ rules His church through a plurality of godly men. He qualifies these men by giving them spiritual gifts and prepares them to serve in the local congregation. The principle task of the pastor is three-fold:

---

[1] John MacArthur, *The Master's Plan for the Church* (Chicago, IL: Moody, 2008), 87.

[2] See also Acts 20:17, 28; Phil 1:1; 1 Tim 3:1; 5:17; Tit 1:5-9).

[3] For an excellent defense of the complementarian view being espoused here see Piper and Grudem, *Recovering Biblical Manhood and Womanhood.*

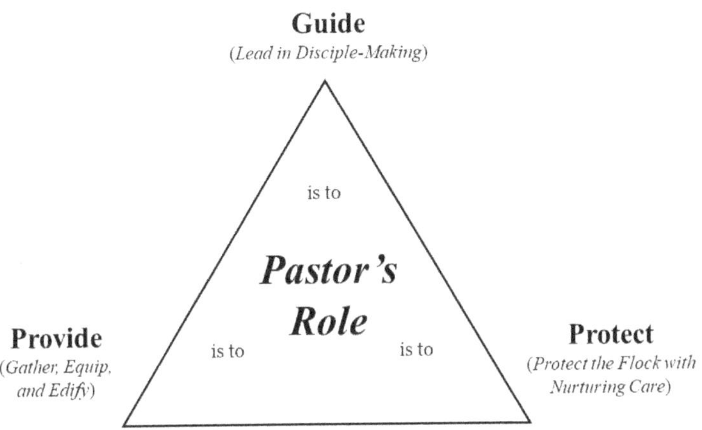

1. Leading in Disciple-Making (Guide). The task of the church is to make disciples (Mt 28:18-20). As noted in chapter two, a pastor's purpose is to lead God's people in this task while demonstrating what a life of sacrifice for Christ looks like. Expounding Hebrews 13:7, "Remember those who rule over you," John MacArthur rightly comments, "In other words, the congregation is spiritually accountable to the elders, and the elders are accountable to God.

2. Gathering-Equipping-Edifying (Provide). Disciple-making is the task of the church. To that end the church, as the pillar and ground of truth, declares the God's will to the world by preaching and teaching the gospel. As Christ's undershepherds, pastors are to lead the congregation's evangelistic efforts, feeding others with God's Word, enabling others to discover their gifts and make disciples who will make disciples (Eph 4:11-12; 1 Tim 4:6-11; 13, 16; 2 Tim 4:2-4; Tit 1:9; 2:1).

3. Protect the Flock with Nurturing Care (Protect). The pastor is to guard the purity of the flock by discerning and shielding them from erroneous teachings and influences (Acts 20: 28-31).

Pastors

While both men and women are gifted for service in the church, the church offices of Elder and Deacon are limited to men as qualified by Scripture. The following qualifications are God's requirements for elders and pastors (preaching elders). The principle texts are: 1 Tim 3:1-7 and Tit 1:6-9.

1. He is blameless (1 Tim 3:2, 10; Tit 1:6, 7).
2. He is the husband of one wife (1 Tim 3:2; Tit 1:6).
3. He is temperate (1 Tim 3:2; Tit 2:1).
4. He is sober-minded (1 Tim 3:2; Tit 1:8).
5. He is of good behavior (1 Tim 3:2).
6. He is hospitable (1 Tim 3:2; Tit 1:8).
7. He is able to teach (1 Tim 3:2).
8. He is not addicted to wine (1 Tim 3:3, 8; Titus 1:7).
9. He is not violent (1 Tim 3:3; Tit 1:7).
10. He is not greedy for money (1 Tim 3:3; Tit 1:7).
11. He is gentle (1 Tim 3:3).
12. He is not covetous (1 Tim 3:3).
13. He rules his own house well (1 Tim 3:4).
14. He has believing children that are under control (1 Tim 3:4; Tit 1:6).
15. He is not a new convert (1 Tim 3:6).
16. He has a good reputation outside the church (1 Tim 3:7).
17. He is not self-willed (Tit 1:7).
18. He is not quick-tempered (Tit 1:7).

19. He loves what is good (Tit 1:8).
20. He is just (Tit 1:8).
21. He is holy (Tit 1:8).
22. He is self-controlled (Tit 1:8).
23. He holds to the faithful word (Titus 1:9).
24. He is able to exhort with sound doctrine and refute those who contradict (Tit 1:9).

Deacons

The early church was faced with the need to provide men who could assume the leading role of serving and caring for the people, specifically the widows and orphans. The term deacon comes to us from the Greek word meaning 'servant,' 'or one who serves.' Acts chapter six tells us that seven men who were "full of the Spirit" were selected among the congregation so the apostles would be free to minister in the Word and prayer. Likewise, the Book of Acts shows us that as local churches were established and grew, deacons were elected among the congregation to assist the elders so they could give themselves to teaching and prayer.

God gifts and calls men to serve as deacons in the local church which confirms and ordains them to the task of administrating and caring for the flock. Some deacons also serve as 'trustees.' The only passage that mentions the qualifications for deacons is 1 Tim 3:8-13. Here are the nine that are listed:

1. Reverent (v. 8): They must have dignity and be worthy of respect. Never treating serious things lightly.

2. Not double-tongued (v. 8): Those who are double-tongued are two-faced and insincere. Their words cannot be trusted, so they lack credibility.

3. Not given to much wine (v. 8): deacons must be self-controlled and disciplined, so as to not give themselves over to addiction to wine or other strong drink.

4. Not greedy for money (v. 8): This is especially important because deacons are normally responsible for handling funds. A man who has a pervasive desire for financial gain is disqualified.

5. Hold the Mystery of the Faith with a clear conscience (v. 9): He must hold conviction from solid biblical truth and apply it daily.

6. Blameless (v. 10): Paul writes that deacons must "be tested first; then let them serve as deacons if they prove themselves blameless" (v. 10). "Blameless" is a general term referring to a person's overall character. Although Paul does not specify what type of testing is to take place, at a minimum, the candidate's personal background, reputation, and theological positions should be examined.

7. Godly wife (v. 11): According to Paul, deacons' wives must "be reverent, not slanderers, but temperate, faithful in all things" (v. 11). Like her husband, the wife must be dignified or respectable. Secondly, she must not be a slanderer or a person who goes around spreading gossip. A deacon's wife must also be sober-minded or temperate. That is, she must be able to make good judgments and must not be involved in things

that might hinder such judgment. Finally, she must be "faithful in all things" (cf. 1 Tim. 5:10).

8. Husband of one wife (v. 12): He must be a "one-woman man." That is, there must be no other woman in his life to whom he relates in an intimate way either emotionally or physically.

9. Manage children and household well (v. 12): A deacon must be the spiritual leader of his wife and children. This qualification affirms the consistent biblical teaching on male leadership in the home.[4]

The demands made of deacons are more of a general variety. Deacons are to administrate, shepherd, and care for the local church. Ridderbos writes, "It is to be gathered from the remainder of the New Testament that the office of deacon especially provided for (the direction of) mutual assistance in the church and will therefore have had reference in particular to what Paul describes in Romans 12 as the charisma of serving, sharing, showing mercy (vv. 6-8), and in 1 Corinthians 12:28 as the gift given by God to the church of the "capacity to help" (*antilempseis*)."[5]

Self-Watch

As we lead others, we must ensure that we don't live in the very sins we preach against (1 Cor 9:27). We must watch our lives and doctrine closely. Persevering in them, because if we do, we will save both ourselves and

---

[4] MacArthur, The Master's Plan for the Church, 257.
[5] Ridderbos, Paul: An Outline of His Theology, 459.

our hearers (1 Tim 4:16). We must ensure that our example doesn't contradict our doctrine. The doctrines we preach must first have worked their power in our own lives. As John Owen once put it, "If it doesn't dwell with power in us, it will not pass with power from us." Similarly, Richard Baxter once observed, "If we would be skillful in governing others, we must learn first to command ourselves." We must ensure that the work of grace be thoroughly accomplished in your own soul, as Paul writes to "work out your own salvation with fear and trembling; for it is God who works in you both to will and to do for His good pleasure" (Phil 2:12-13).

The most radical social teaching of Jesus was His total reversal of the contemporary notion of greatness. Leadership is found in becoming the servant of all. Power is discovered in submission; the foremost symbol of this radical servanthood is the cross. Jesus flatly rejected the cultural givens of position and power when He said "You are not to be called Rabbi... neither called masters."[6] Biblical leadership is influencing others by providing purpose, direction, and motivation to live obedient lives for Christ.

When God calls men to lead His people, He is not looking for those who feel sufficient to the task but for those who are faithful. Thus, as we lead others, we are to always remember we are God's work from beginning to end. God makes use of means to mold us into the instruments for His glory. Preachers are no different. And there is nothing juicier to the devil that to destroy the ministry of one of Christ's under shepherds. Leaders, we must ensure that we are not only in a state of grace, but daily vigorously exercise that grace.

---

[6] Foster, Celebration of Discipline, 101.

Leaders perform many tasks, often times that are unpopular in the culture in which they live. However, God calls His leaders not to be popular but to be faithful. As such, God uses the lives of His leaders to challenge their culture and call them to repentance and faith in Jesus Christ. Ultimately, the litmus test of leadership is not popularity, it is faithfulness.

The following discussion surveys leaders from the Old and New Testaments. The life and leadership of each of these leaders holds out to us both failures to avoid as well as examples to follow.

Gideon: A Leader with a Weak Finish

Regarding leadership, Gideon provides some commendable things as well as things to avoid. Gideon's leadership is rightly described by Don Howell as divine power in human weakness.[7] In all, God gave Israel twelve Judges: Gideon was the fifth. As Judges 6:1 tells us, "The people of Israel did what was evil in the sight of the Lord," and a new generation repeated the same mistakes of their fathers and turned to the seductive pleasures of the Canaanites. Again, God sold the people into the hands of their enemies, this time the Midianites (Judges 6:6). But God was merciful and raised up a deliverer, the unlikely hero, Gideon.

Gideon was the son of Joash, the Abiezrite, who of all things, was the village priest of Baal (Judges 6:25). Israel had been brought so low that they had to hide their sustenance. And when God came to raise up Israel's deliverer, Gideon is found threshing wheat in a

---

[7] Don N. Howell, *Servants of the Servant: A Biblical Theology of Leadership* (Eugene, OR: Wipf & Stock, 2003), 53.

winepress (Judges 6:11-14). Ironically, God announces to Gideon "The Lord is with you, O mighty man of valor"! This teaches us: Like all spiritual leaders, God looks at Gideon and sees the man He is going to make out of him (Rom 4:17). Initially, like Moses, Gideon resists God's call but is sufficiently encouraged to take up God's summons.

Gideon is zealous for God to be exalted in His redemptive work. But in Gideon we find a man who is very unsure of himself.[8] He is a man who is very much in doubt. He exhibits both faith and fear.[9] God could have used whomever He wanted. He could have chosen someone mighty but He chose someone weak and insignificant; someone hopeless enough that He would use for His glory (Judges 7:2; 1 Cor 1:27).

God's deliverance begins with the restoration of true worship. In preparation for holy war, Gideon must make a clean break with his past and consecrate himself wholly to the Lord's service. As instructed by God, Gideon tears down his father's altar of Baal along with the Asherah pole beside it. He then built in their place an altar at which worship may be made to the God of Israel (Judges 6:25-26). The real problem in Israel was not the presence of the Midianites, but idolatry. And once worship is renewed an army is assembled. Gideon is nonetheless still far from what one would call a valiant warrior but God is incredibly patient with Gideon's weak faith, and graciously gives him two signs involving a fleece to build up his weak faith. Then the Spirit of God came upon Gideon, and he was clothed with mighty power.

---

[8] Benjamin K. Forrest and Chet Roden, *Biblical Leadership: Theology for the Everyday Leader* (Grand Rapids, MI: Kregel, 2017), 103.
[9] Ibid.

Then by a process of elimination, first from 32,000 down to 10,000 for those afraid, the Lord whittled down Gideon's 'army' to a mere 300 men. Then at midnight, Gideon's army surrounds the sleeping Midianite horde in three companies, and with a combination of blowing trumpets, broken jars, piercing light, and the shout of victory, the Midianites are completely surprised and conclude that a vast host of Israelite warriors have surrounded them. And as "the Lord set every man's sword against his companion," the enemy force proceeded to hack each other to bits; the survivors made their way to the fords of the Jordan (Judges 7:22).

Great victory brought great fame, and Gideon was invited to be Israel's king (Judges 8:22). Although he wisely refused, in an ironic twist of tragedy, Gideon brought Israel back into idolatry by making a golden ephod made from war plunder (Judges 8:24-27; Ex 32:1-4). Though he rejected the kingship, he began increasingly to act like an ancient near eastern king; having seventy sons by his many wives, and of course much gold; thus, violating the command of Deuteronomy 17:14-20 (Judges 8:29).[10]

Gideon's life and leadership reminds the church of at least three positive lessons and one negative lesson. The biblical account of Gideon is very encouraging for believers because it shows that God would choose a man very weak in himself to be a leader. This is because God is not put off by or limited by weaknesses. God doesn't say well this one doesn't have a good enough background, or good enough education, rather God's strength is perfected in weakness (2 Cor 12:10).

---

[10] Ibid., 104.

Positively (1) God invests His purpose in leaders who are weak and imperfect, so that in victory, His glory is more clearly displayed (2 Cor 12:9); (2) it is what God says of us that makes us who we are. God says from the beginning who He is going to make us (Rom 4:17); and (3) As leaders, we are to go forth in the power and zeal that God supplies and the battle is the Lord's (Zech 4:6).

Negatively, we may take note from Gideon's weak finish as a leader that "pride is the leader's constant enemy."[11] Tellingly, Gideon's shout of victory at the battle had been "the sword of the Lord, *and of Gideon*" (Judges 7:20; emphasis added). Gideon's victory was thus tainted with pride.12 Ultimately, as a spiritual leader, Gideon failed because he led people away from the true worship of God.

David: Let God Defend You

After Israel's Judges, came the time of Israel's kings. David, Israel's second king, was brought up on the countryside of Bethlehem shepherding his father's sheep. As a young man, he walked very close with God and depended not on his weapons but on God, and God used him to defeat Goliath and defend Israel. Later David became a general in Saul's Army, relying not on his weapons but on God. He then became the king's son-in-law and before all of this he had been anointed to be Israel's next king. And due to David's obedient life and success, Saul became insanely jealous and tried

[11] Ibid.
[12] Ibid.

to kill him on at least ten occasions. David then became an outcast and an outlaw and ran for his life.

Being hard pressed, David began to backslide away from the presence of God. He said to his friend Jonathan, Saul's son: "there is but a step between me and death" (1 Sam 20:3). David backslides because his situation in life becomes more dominate and real to him then the promises of God. David had great faith facing the giant Goliath but now he is running from Saul and has forgotten the promises of God and can see only his present plight. David got into trouble when he became more concerned with his physical welfare than his spiritual welfare.

Something the life and leadership of David teaches us is this: The way back into conscious fellowship with God is through a broken heart. And David repents and is restored. Then "everyone who was in distress, everyone who was in debt, and everyone who was discontented gathered to him. So, he became captain over them, and "there were about four hundred men with him" (1 Sam 22:1-2). A leadership lesson here is: Once you walk with God, the people who walk with God will find you and follow you.

Hounded by Saul, David and his band narrowly escape many times. Then on one occasion, David has an opportunity to kill Saul while the king is asleep (1 Sam 26). Though David's men encourage him to kill Saul, David understands something every leader should: God rules the universe and there is no authority that exists that He has not put in place; the authority and exercise of all human leadership flows from God (Rom 13:1-7).[13] David knew that if God

---

[13] Ibid., 39.

anointed him to rule, then it was God's prerogative to bring it about in His time, not David's. And in time, God raised David up to reign in Israel after God brought an end to Saul. There are many principles from the life and leadership of David: (1) leaders must see God's promises as more real than anything else; (2) leaders are to be true, and let God defend them (Rom 12:19-21); and (3) one who leads, must do so with diligence (Rom 12:8).

Jeremiah: With God, One is in the Majority

Jeremiah was born somewhere towards the end of the 50-year reign of Manasseh, who was the worst and most wicked kings that ever sat on the throne of Judah. Some 20 years before Manasseh took the throne of Judah in 721 BC, the 10 northern tribes were taken away into the Assyrian captivity and ceased to exist as a nation. It was at this time that Judah entered its darkest hour, and at that time God called Jeremiah to lead as a prophet. And the word of the Lord came to Jeremiah and said: "Before I formed you in the womb I knew you; before you were born I sanctified you; I ordained you a prophet to the nations" (Jer 1:5).

A leadership lesson we learn here is: As God called and commissioned Jeremiah and assured him that He will not abandon him, God does for all His leaders. This is encouraging because Jeremiah's ministry was very unpopular and caused him to be out of sync with society. In fact, Jeremiah's ministry got him into a lot great trouble. And when Jeremiah was faced with trials, he had to go back to God's call upon his life. God gave him the promise that He would be with him in the thick of the trouble and would not abandon him.

Likewise, when leaders are faced with trouble or depression, they must go back to their calling.

The essence of Jeremiah's message is surrender your whole life to God and He will give you a future and a hope; "Only acknowledge your iniquity, that you have transgressed against the Lord your God" (Jer 3:13). Jeremiah wasn't the only preacher around. There were false prophets saying we have the temple and we have the right political dealings, everything is great. There were many preachers in those days who were preaching a popular message but we do not even have their names. Jeremiah's preaching was so unpopular that he incurred the people's wrath and they threaten his life and he suffered confinement and deprivation.[14]

Jeremiah laments his situation and the Lord replied by asking Jeremiah how he expected to be able to endure the rigors of coming antagonism if the present hostility he was experiencing wore him out. The Lord said: "If you have run with the footmen, and they have wearied you, then how can you contend with horses" (Jer 12:5)? In other words, if relatively small problems (like having your life threatened for the gospel) knock you over, what will you do when you face big ones? Likewise, as ministers of the gospel and leaders of Christ's church, we must expect faithfulness to God's Word to be met by tribulation and persecution (Jn 16:33; 2 Tim 3:12).

Jeremiah's life and leadership teach us at least three major principles: (1) With God, one person is in the majority (Rom 8:31); (2) It is God's authority, not your own, that is behind your leadership (Rom 13:1); and (3)

---

[14] Ibid., 196.

God Himself will be with you to deliver you in all your trials (Zech 3:9; 1 Pet 5:10).

The Old Testament prophesies, prefigured and foreshadows everything that Jesus Christ fulfills. And in the fulness of time, God sent His Son to embody everything these Old Testament leaders foreshadowed and prefigured. Whereas Gideon stood as a type of Christ, who delivered God's people from bondage, Christ conquered our enemies of sin and death, and freed us from our deadly foe. As David pointed to Christ our King, when Jesus was reviled, He did not revile in return but instead He trusted Himself to Him who judges justly. That is, He handed over His grievance to God and let the Father defend Him. Why? Because Jesus was showing us that vengeance is God's prerogative (Rom 12:19). And Jeremiah pointed the way to the Savior in that he suffered unjustly at the hands of those he desired to save, as all God's leaders will do.

Gideon, David and Jeremiah were all servants of God, who, in varying ways, pointed the way to the perfect Leader of God's people, Jesus Christ, who we are to imitate (1 Cor 11:1).

Coming now to the New Testament, we move to discuss a leader of the Early Church: Stephen. The life and leadership of Stephen encourages us to follow his example by fearlessly confronting our culture with the truth about God, the truth about the world and the truth about ourselves. The life and leadership of Stephen teaches us at least three principles: (1) leaders must accurately handle the Word of God; (2) leaders must understand that results in ministry does not ultimately depend on them; and (3) leaders must be driven not by fads but by conviction. An understanding of these principles is crucial to Christian leadership.

Stephen: The Prophetic Voice of Truth

There was once a young missionary named David Brainerd who lived in the early 1700s. He had a huge impact on missions but died at the youthful age of twenty-nine. What's remarkable was how he made such a big impact. He had been a missionary to Native Americans, particularly the Delaware Indians of New Jersey, but he got sick and spent his last days in the house of Jonathan Edwards, the pastor God used to spark the Great Awakening, the first great revival in the United States. As he lay dying, Edwards took down his memoires which were later found itself into print entitled the *Dairies of David Brainerd*. And that book would be one of the most incredible catalysts for missionary activity over the next 150 years.

Likewise, what we find in the life of Stephen, is a life cut short but a life that served as the catalyst for missionary activity in the Early Church. In fact, God providentially uses Stephen's speech and martyrdom to bring the gospel outside of Jerusalem and take it, as He said, to Judea, Samaria, and the uttermost parts of the earth (Acts 1:8; 8:1). Stephen's life and leadership had enormous theological and missionary impact.

As a leader, Stephen was God's prophetic voice of truth and his example is exemplary. Regardless of the danger, he embraced the call and stood as one with God against the majority.[15]

---

[15] Ibid., 370.

Similar to the prophets of old, Stephen's indictment is against the apostate leaders of Israel, the priests, rulers, and false prophets (Acts 7:51-53; cf. Jer 2:8). God contended with the unfaithful ways of Israel, who broke His covenant. The people of Jerusalem did not believe that judgment would befall them. Why? Because they had an "edifice complex." They reasoned because they had the temple no judgment would befall them.

Likewise, the people of Jerusalem in Stephen's day were still formally following the religion of the covenant, they were showing up at the feasts, but their hearts were not in it. The attitude of the people was "We are Abraham's offspring." And as God's covenant prosecutor, Stephen brought charges against her. Stephen's words enacted the covenant curse for unfaithfulness: sword, famine, and pestilence (Jer 14:12; Lev 26:14-44).

Stephen accurately handled the Word and said: "Which one of the prophets did your fathers not persecute? And they killed those who foretold the coming of the Just One" (Acts 7:52). The people's refusal to acknowledge Jesus as the Messiah was in keeping with their rejection of the prophets before Him. By these words, God's caused His people to lose land, temple, people and city. Yet, while God's Word brings judgment and death, it also brings restoration and rebuilding through repentance (Acts 2:39; Jer 21:8-10).

After this indictment, Stephen stood in trial before the Sanhedrin. And when he gave his defense, it was not designed to secure his acquittal, rather it was a defense of the truth. A defense of the gospel not himself. The essence of Stephen's argument was: the presence of God is not restricted to any one land or any material building, and citing Isaiah 66:1-2, Stephen reminded his listeners that God is unlimited in His nature and presence. Like Jeremiah, Stephen stood against the many. But with God, one man is in the majority. Full of the Holy Spirit, Stephen fearlessly confronted his culture with the gospel and depended upon God's power to bring results. He led through weakness, vulnerability, and self-sacrifice.[16]

The life and leadership of Stephen teaches us that God calls His leaders to be the prophetic voice of truth to our culture. Along with the other leaders in the Early Church, Stephen knew that his source of truth and authority was God's Word and Spirit, and not their personalities, powers of persuasion or philosophy. As leaders, God has called us to fearlessly confront our culture with the gospel and God will bring about the result (Mt 10:32-29).

Leadership may be summed up by the word "influence." There are essentially four principles of Christian leadership: **LEAD**

L – Led by the Holy Spirit (Teach as you are taught)
E – Example (Lead by example)
A – Accountability (Be open and humble)
D – Doctrine (Preach and teach the apostolic doctrine)

(1) It is the church's responsibility to follow-up and disciple new converts to bring them to maturity; (2) It is the church's responsibility to facilitate small groups for discipleship; (3) It is the church's responsibility to facilitate leadership training.

[16] Ibid., 349.

Chapter Twelve:
Disciple-Making

"Discipleship is not an option. Jesus says that if anyone would come after me, he must follow me." – Tim Keller

The mission of the Church is to make disciples. Jesus commanded us: "Go therefore and make disciples of all the nations, baptizing them in the name of the Father and of the Son and of the Holy Spirit, teaching them to observe all things that I have commanded you" (Mt 28:19-20).

What passes for disciple-making these days? Having some coffee before worship? Taking part in a small group? Going through a new members class? All such modes of interaction and instruction sharing can be beneficial, albeit do they really pass for biblical disciple-making? What often takes place in these modes of fellowship is new believers are never really known or discipled. In this chapter, our goal will be to define what a disciple is and how disciple-making is to be done.

What is a Disciple?

The word "disciple," in the Greek μαθητής *mathetes* means learner. The disciples of Jesus followed Him and learned from Him. A disciple is therefore a learner and follower of Jesus. A disciple also imitates the Christ-like character of another, such as when Timothy was discipled by the Apostle Paul. Essentially, there are four characteristics of a disciple of Jesus: Knows, grows, shows and goes. First, a disciple "knows" Jesus by trusting in Him for salvation and has surrendered completely to Him. Second, a disciple "grows" in Jesus by committing to the practice of spiritual disciplines in the Church and developing to their full potential for Christ and His mission.[1] Third, as an image-bearer of Jesus, a disciple "shows" Jesus to others. And fourth, a disciple is someone who "goes" for Jesus, joining Him on His mission.

To begin with, a disciple is a person who "knows" Jesus. In other words, every believer is a disciple of Jesus. A Christian and a disciple of Jesus are one and the same thing. As the first characteristic, a disciple is someone who has trusted in Jesus Christ for salvation and has surrendered completely to Him. This is a radical commitment. In Luke chapter nine, Jesus declares the radical cost of following Him. Luke 9:57-62 tells us:

> 57 Now it happened as they journeyed on the road, that someone said to Him, "Lord, I will follow You wherever You go." 58 And Jesus said to him, "Foxes have holes and birds of the air have nests, but the Son of Man has nowhere to lay His head." 59 Then He said to another, "Follow Me." But he said, "Lord, let me first go and bury my father." 60 Jesus said to him, "Let the dead bury their own dead, but you go and preach the kingdom of God." 61 And another also said, "Lord, I will follow You, but let me first go and bid them farewell who are at my house." 62 But Jesus said to him, "No one, having put his hand to the plow, and looking back, is fit for the kingdom of God."

---

[1] Dave Earley and Rod Dempsey, *Disciple Making Is: How to Live the Great Commission with Passion and Confidence* (Nashville, TN: B&H Academic, 2013), 39.

Important to bear in mind is Luke chapter nine is all about Jesus going to the cross; "He steadfastly set His face to go to Jerusalem" (Lk 9:51). Knowing this is what led Dietrich Bonhoeffer to observe: "When Christ calls a man, He bids him come and die."[2] In Luke 9:57-62, we have three would-be disciples who underestimated the degree of commitment that Jesus requires. The text also provides three distinctives regarding the centrality of Christ in discipleship: Lordship, life and likeness. Jesus is to be first in all things (Col 1:18). This is part of what Jesus means when He said: "Foxes have holes and birds of the air have nests, but the Son of Man has nowhere to lay His head" (Lk 9:56). This is a call to abandon self-reliance and to take one's hands off the helm of life.

Following Jesus as His disciple therefore involves a great deal of uncertainty. Surrendering to Christ is to be unconditional.[3] There are to be no areas of a disciple's life that are not surrendered to Christ's lordship. One's mind, will and emotions are all to be given up to Christ as a living sacrifice (Rom 12:1). Discipleship is the lifelong relationship with Jesus whereby a disciple surrenders all of life to Jesus. Following Jesus begins by giving up everything (Lk 9:57).

Second, a disciple "grows" in Christ, as the centrality of Christ requires living solely for Him (Lk 9:60).[4] In other words, following Jesus has moral significance. Jesus said: "If you love Me, obey My commandments" (Jn 14:15). In Luke 9:23-24, Jesus sums up this

---

[2] Ibid., 89.
[3] Dietrich Bonhoeffer, *The Cost of Discipleship* (New York: Simon & Schuster, 1959), 61.
[4] Ibid., 56.

distinctive: "If anyone desires to come after Me, let him deny himself, and take up his cross daily, and follow Me. For whoever desires to save his life will lose it, but whoever loses his life for My sake will save it." A disciple grows in Christ committing to the practice of spiritual disciplines such as: Worship, prayer, Scripture reading and meditation, fasting, giving, acts of service, witnessing the gospel, etc. (Mt 6).

Christian Discipleship is a spiritual journey that involves following Christ. By Christ's design, disciples are to grow and mature. As anyone who has served in the ministry long enough knows, there are many believers "who have remained stagnant in their faith" and remain spiritual infants (Heb 5:12). Disciples grow in grace as they follow Christ's example in the Wilderness: When to tempted to sin, the pleasure of the sin offered must be denied. This process of growing in grace begins when the call to new life is given and in fact never ends this side of eternity (Lk 9:57-62). It is for this reason that Dietrich Bonhoeffer rightly said, "Discipleship is inseparable from grace."[5] The point is, disciples are not perfect, nor will they be this side of heaven. Nonetheless, God's standard is "be holy as I am holy" (1 Pet 1:16). And God forgives our lack of being perfect by accepting us in Christ.

Third, disciples are called to be God's image bearers, to bear the image of Jesus Christ to the world. A disciple therefore "shows" Jesus to the world. As a disciple grows in grace, they are to increasingly bear Christ's image. Disciples are to love as Jesus loved (Jn 13:35). Discipleship is taking place as believers obey Christ and allow themselves to be transformed into

---

[5] Dietrich Bonhoeffer, *The Cost of Discipleship*, 51, 55, 56, and 59.

Christ's image. This is not automatic. It requires a disciple to be under the lordship of Christ, surrendering all areas of life to Him. Knowing that the old life is crucified with Christ, the life of the disciple is to exemplify obedience in all areas, whether at home, at work, at church; everywhere (Gal 2:20-21).

Fourth, disciples are to make other disciples, going with Jesus on His mission. Disciples are to be like Jesus in life and ministry, keeping their hands on the plow, serving in that part of the Vineyard that Christ put them in (Lk 9:62). Christ saves and calls His people into a fellowship with Himself and His saints (1 Cor 1:9). All Christians are therefore disciples who, by Christ's design, are to be equipped for service within the fellowship of the local church. There are to be no "Lone Ranger" Christians (Heb 10:25). The church is absolutely essential for disciple-making because it is in the local church that we are equipped and taught. It therefore takes a church to make disciples.

What is Disciple-Making?

Disciples are made in the local church by the power of the gospel through three imperatives: Leadership, accountability and relationships. The word 'disciple' *mathetes* μαθητής according to Merrill Unger is, "one who professes to have learned certain principles from another and maintains them on that other's authority."[6] Christ determined the place of discipleship was to be within the gathered community of believers.

---

[6] Merrill Unger, *Unger's Bible Dictionary* (Chicago: Moody Press, 1957), 265.

Jesus' method of making disciples was that He first "shared who He was through words and deeds."[7]

Likewise, by Christ's design, the Church shares who Jesus is through the gospel. This takes place corporately and individually as it is mediated through godly church leadership, that is, through pastors, elders, deacons, and lay leaders, in whatever program or outreach and at whatever home group or other time of fellowship where Christians meet. Among other things, leaders ensure the core doctrines of the Christian faith is taught, along with delegating service opportunities and supervising programs within the church.[8]

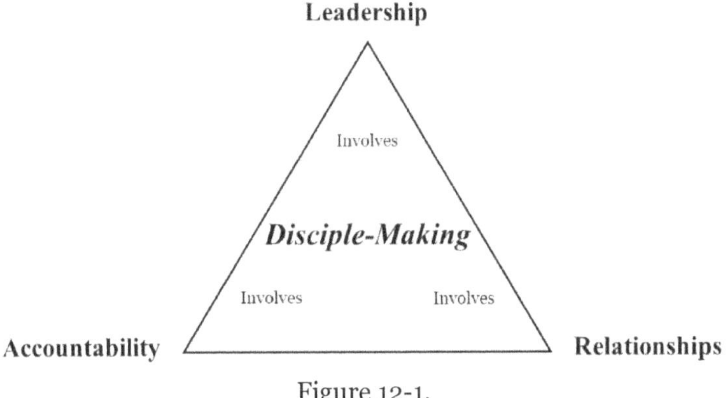

Figure 12-1.

First, leadership in the church is imperative to disciple-making and encompasses three convictions: (1) It is the church's responsibility to follow-up and disciple new converts to bring them to maturity; (2) It

---

[7] Jim Putman, *Discipleshift: Five Steps That Help Your Church to Make Disciples Who Make Disciples* (Grand Rapids: Zondervan, 2013), 153.
[8] Ibid., 160.

is the church's responsibility to facilitate small groups for discipleship; (3) It is the church's responsibility to facilitate leadership training.[9] Whatever the mode, disciple-making occurs in the local church as church leaders teach and emphasize the necessity for the whole body of Christ to participate in disciple-making. The role of pastors in this is to invigorate the life of the church by equipping others, so that disciple-making will occur.[10]

Disciple-making can go on within the church without leadership, albeit less effectively as pastors not only shape what the congregation believes, they also model it and encourage the discipling of others. As Bonhoeffer once noted, "leaders facilitate disciple-making in the local congregation as others see them live out the Christian life and others see them do it."[11]

As a second imperative, disciple-making also involves discipline and accountability. In order for disciple-making to happen within the church, believers have to be accountable to God's Word, His spiritual leaders, and each other in the local congregation (Eph 5:18; Heb 13:17). Perhaps one of the biggest detriments to disciple-making in the church today is caused by a lack of accountability? Americans today seem to be overly sensitive and too individualistic. Both of which are barriers to disciple-making. Accountability is therefore reciprocal to discipleship. No accountability, no disciple-making. Accountability is imperative to

---

[9] Mark R. Shaw, *Ten Great Ideas from Church History: A Decision-Maker's Guide to Shaping Your Church* (Downers Grove, IL: IVP, 1997), 136.

[10] Ibid.

[11] Dietrich Bonhoeffer, *The Cost of Discipleship* (New York: Simon & Schuster, 1959), 153.

holy living (1 Pet 1:16). Christians must be accountable to each other if there is ever to be any genuine growth toward spiritual maturity (Pro 27:17; Gal 6:2, 5).

It may be said that everyone who has fallen in their Christian walk has failed to be accountable in some way. Many, who, confident of their own spiritual arrivedness, have fallen in an extra-marital affair or a financial conundrum. Without accountability, a fall is not far off. Accountability is therefore an imperative of disciple-making. Accountability is often thought to be a Puritanical practice for kill joys. However, as Stu Weber observes, "The thrust of accountability is not meant to be punitive, but preventative. [12] Every believer (disciple of Jesus) needs the accountability that comes from intimate relationships with other godly people.[13]

The third imperative for disciple-making is relationships. It may be asked: Why does accountability proceed relationships? It does because believers that have not held themselves accountable to God's Word and each other in the local congregation cannot really experience genuine fellowship with God's people. Fellowship with the local church is a test that many fail. Those who have a personal relationship with Christ are to have relationships with Christ's people. It is these relationships that will enable the believer to persevere for the long haul. For, it is within Christian relationships that disciple-making primarily takes place within the local church.[14]

---

[12] Stu Weber, *Locking Arms: God's Design for Masculine Friendships* (Colorado Springs, CO: Multnomah, 1995), 162.
[13] Wayne A. Mack, *To Be or Not to Be a Church Member* (Ashland, OH: Calvary Press, 2007), 64.
[14] Jim Putman, *Discipleshift*, 134.

Disciple-making is facilitated by leadership and accountability but cannot have real meaning without relationship (Rom 15:4; Col 3:16; Heb 3:13; Jude 1:20). Echoing this point, John MacArthur observes, "Discipleship is nothing more than building a true friendship with a spiritual basis. It's not being friends with someone because you both like the same sport, the same music, the same hobbies, or work at the same place. At the core of your friendship should be openness about spiritual issues, which will carry your discipling relationship along."[15]

The prerequisite for spiritual relationships is first a genuine love for the other less spiritually mature believer, and second, a genuine desire for to be discipled. The less mature believer in fact may not necessarily realize they are being discipled. Nonetheless, disciple-making is still taking place.

As the Word of God is taught and lived out by more mature disciples, less mature disciples learn and apply the lessons to their lives (1 Cor 11:1). Thus, God, making use of means, works to purify His saints. Two are better than one. Believers are strengthened and become more like Christ through spiritual relationship within the local congregation: "As iron sharpens iron, so a man sharpens the countenance of his friend" (Pro 27:17). Thus, fellowship is essential to become more like Christ.

Christ is purifying for Himself His own special people who are made zealous for good works (Titus 2:14). God is bringing many sons to glory out of every tribe and tongue and people and nation and He has

---

[15] John MacArthur, *The Master's Plan for the Church* (Chicago: Moody, 2008), 67-68.

been gathering His own since history began, calling them to live in a covenant fellowship with Himself and His people – the church, which is the pillar and ground of truth (1 Cor 1:9; 1 Tim 3:15; Rev 5:9). Discipleship is to be within the context of fellowship in the local church, because you cannot make a disciple without God's means of grace (Acts 2:41-42).

There are some rather disturbing modern trends in our churches today. Even if our church abstains from the seeker-sensitive, entertainment model of doing church, there is a trend in many churches of having newcomers ascent to an abstract doctrinal system, become a baptized member of a congregation, then give their tithe and some of their time. However, this renders discipleship superfluous. While it is possible to have formal knowledge, be enthusiastic about it, and even put some of it into practice, an abstract doctrine can never be followed in personal obedience.[16] It is not possible for believers to grow in an environment of mere formal knowledge being broadcast to them two times a week at best. What this system organically produces is believers who never make it out of the spiritual infant stage.[17]

We will live out what we believe. We need doctrine to frame our lives but we also need holy relationships. Mankind was made to live in relationships. Abstract ideas are therefore only put into practice by intentional examples provided by life-on-life discipleship. For a church to function according to Christ's design, "Go and make disciples," it must practice intentional one-on-one, life-on-life discipleship (Mt 28:18; 1 Cor 11:1).

---

[16] Dietrich Bonhoeffer, *The Cost of Discipleship*, 59.

[17] Ibid.

On Paul's second missionary journey (49-51 AD), when his team reached the cities of Derby and Lystra, they met up with Timothy, who we are told was "a certain disciple," of Jesus (Acts 16:1). Paul invited Timothy to join him and become his disciple. In other words, Paul invited Timothy to imitate him as he (Paul) imitated Christ (1 Cor 11:1). Whenever Paul taught, his disciples listened, learning from him what and how to preach and teach. They learned how to lead and whenever Paul was persecuted, they learned how he persevered. It was during this time, accompanying the Apostle Paul, that Timothy no doubt learned how to serve in numerous menial tasks such as buying travel tickets, cooking meals, washing clothes, packing baggage, and making tents. But in the process, he was being trained to be a man of God. In this way, Paul was multiplying himself in the life of Timothy.

Later, when Paul was confined to prison, he sent Titus to Crete, Timothy to Ephesus, and Epaphroditus to Colossae, along with others to different places. Paul's discipleship training over the years in the lives of these other men made them extensions of himself.[18] This of course is the Lord's pattern of disciple-making. Jesus took everyday men who were "uneducated and untrained" from various backgrounds, poured Himself into their lives for three and half years, and through the power of His Spirit in them, turned the world upside down. And as they did, the world realized it was because "they had been with Jesus" (Acts 4:13).

Likewise, pastors are to lead the church in disciple-making, in a full commitment to the Great Commission. Pastors are to be intentional in the

---

[18] Ibid., 154.

making of disciples for Christ, feeding others with the Word of God while demonstrating what a life that is fully surrendered to Christ looks like. When it comes to disciple-making, pastors are to "invest" themselves in the lives of other believers. There are essentially four principles of disciple-making: **REAP**

R – Relationship
E – Example
A – Accountability
P – Progress:

(1) Dependence on God (devotional life, direction and strength).
(2) Christlikeness – Head (thinking), heart (being), hands (doing).
(3) Spiritual gifts (discovery and use).

Chapter Thirteen: Evangelism

"It's the whole business of the whole church to preach the whole gospel to the whole world." – Charles H. Spurgeon

The Great Commission is accomplished through worship, evangelism and disciple-making (Rev 12:11). Rather than being a special task for those specifically gifted, evangelism is the Church's task. Afterall, disciple-making is evangelism. The word evangelism comes to us from the Latin *evangelium*, itself derived from the Greek εὐαγγελίζω *euaggelizo* which means "I bring good news." The derivation of "gospel" is the old English godspel from gōd good + spell tale = good news. Evangelism is therefore the proclamation of the good news. It involves displaying Christ and explaining man's need of Him, Christ's power to save all who truly turn to Him.

In the Book of Acts, we have the history of how the Church began with 120 disciples, and through the Spirit's power, expand beyond its exclusive Jewish viewpoint in Jerusalem, to encompass the Gentiles and spread the message of Christ throughout the Roman Empire, to the ends of the earth. The Book of Acts shows us the apostles faithfully discharging their divine mission to declare the whole council of God and, amongst other things, provides us with a blueprint for biblical evangelism. In this chapter, our goal will be to outline seven principles of evangelism that we have from the Book of Acts:

1. Providence.
2. Prayer.
3. Power.
4. Proclamation.
5. Provision.
6. Persecution.
7. Perseverance.

1. Providence – As the Bible teaches, God upholds, directs, disposes and govern all creatures, actions, and things by His providence for His glory and the good of His Church (Rom 8:28). God's providence is the working out of His own plan through the ordinary circumstances of life. God acts in time and space to bring about the plan He has decreed.

In our evangelistic efforts, we can trust God's providence and His Word. God has a specific number of people who will be His. This is precisely the point the Apostle Paul's makes when he tells Timothy, "The Lord knows those who are His" (2 Tim 2:19).

Some may object to this and reason that such thinking reduces people to robots, circumventing man's will. However, the Bible speaks in terms that God is sovereign and mankind is responsible. Man is a responsible moral agent, though he is also spiritually dead and completely dependent upon God to save him. The Bible's mathematics is 200%. God is 100% sovereign. Job says: "I know that You can do everything, and that no purpose of Yours can be withheld from You" (Job 42:2). And yet man is 100% responsible. Ezekiel declares: "The soul that sins shall die" (Ezek 18:20). Some may object and say why evangelize at all? Rather than think this way, God's sovereignty gives us confidence that our labor in the

Lord is not in vain, and that as we proclaim the gospel, Christ's sheep will be saved.

In evangelism, as J.I. Packer observes, "God's way of saving men is to send out His servants to tell them the gospel, and the Church has been charged to go into all the world for that very purpose."[1]

The Book of Acts demonstrates the principle of providence from the very beginning. Following His resurrection, the Apostles spent forty days with Jesus being instructed by Him regarding "the things pertaining to the kingdom of God" (Acts 1:3). Then, before He ascended into heaven, Jesus told them not to depart from Jerusalem but to wait for the Promise of the Father, for they would be baptized in the Holy Spirit, and "you shall receive power when the Holy Spirit has come upon you; and you shall be witnesses to Me in Jerusalem, and in all Judea and Samaria, and to the end of the earth" (Acts 1:8).

The apostles weren't told to devise a strategy for world evangelism, they were told to wait. They were told to wait to receive power for service. They were told to wait to receive direction. In light of God's providence, and the fact that the church is God's instrument of evangelism, this first principle of evangelism would have us trust in God's divine orchestration. We are to be confident as we step out in faith to see the lost come to Christ. And the reason we can be confident is, all of Christ's sheep will come to Him. Jesus declared in no uncertain terms: "All that the Father gives Me will come to Me" (Jn 6:37).

---

[1] J. I. Packer, *Evangelism and the Sovereignty of God* (Downers Grove: IVP, 2010), 33.

2. Prayer – What the Book of Acts shows is the Early Church didn't form plans as to how they should appear in public, rather they "continued with one accord in prayer and supplication" (Acts 1:14). Our purpose in prayer is not to inform God or change His plan in some way, rather prayer is a channel through which His ordained plan comes to pass. This is precisely the situation in Acts chapter one. The disciples all prayed for God to do what He had promised. What we learn from this is, we pray to align ourselves with God's will and we pray because God has ordained prayer as one of the means by which He will accomplish His plan.

The Early Church knew they were God's instrument. They were praying for God to use them according to His plan. As Doug Kelly observes, "When we are stuck in some hard situation and are begging God for His revealed will to be brought to pass, we are actually praying that way because God has put us in the position where we will feel the need to pray! Our praying is, in fact, a preparation for the release of the blessings of God."[2]

As we pray in Jesus' name, God receives these prayers and meets with divine acceptance and power (Rev 5:8-11; 8:1-5). God orchestrates His divine appointments and desires for us to have a heart like His for the lost; He wants us to treasure what He treasures. Prayer is a way this takes place. It's God's way of stirring up the hearts of His people.

3. Power – The Church in Acts chapter one constituted the renewed people of God. They had one Lord, one faith and one baptism but they needed power

---

[2] Doug Kelly, *If God Already Knows Why Pray*, 58.

for service (Eph 4:5). They needed God's power to be enabled to bear witness to Christ and his gospel.

When I was a boy, I was glued to the TV set watching the series "Mission Impossible." In that series, a small team of secret agents conducted covert missions against evil organizations. The episodes began when an assignment from a hidden tape recorder said something like: "Your mission, should you decide to accept it" is to save the entire world though the chance you'll survive is one in a million. Then it said: "As always, should you or any of your impossible mission force be caught or killed, the Secretary will disavow any knowledge of your actions." Then the tape went up and smoke.

Likewise, the mission of the Church seems an impossible mission. Jesus said "Now go out now and change the world and turn it upside down." Go and make disciples of all the nations, baptize them, and teach them everything I have commanded you" (Mt 28:18-20). And as you do, Jesus said, you will be hated by everyone, and those who kill you, will do so thinking they offer God service. And the people Jesus sends out to accomplish this mission are simple people, without money, without political power or influence.

Adding to the difficulty, the message they are to bear witness to is about how Yahweh the Creator, the transcendent God of the universe, Who gives us every breath, left the courts of heaven to become a penniless preacher, die for our sins by being crucified naked. Not only that, but these disciples have to go to the Greek and Romans who believe as Plato and Aristotle taught that truth, beauty and justice were cosmic ideals that exist in the immaterial world, they have to go to them and say: Truth exists in a Person whose name is Jesus

Christ. And who is Jesus? He's an executed Person who lived in a backwater part of the world in the Roman colony of Judea.

Now from that perspective, that is truly mission impossible. But Jesus said there is going to be Someone with you on this mission and that makes all the difference in the world. The disciples were already saved and regenerated by the Holy Spirit prior to the "coming" of the Spirit at Pentecost. But they needed the gifts of the Spirit to qualify them for the work they were to do. Christ's gifts are supernatural abilities granted by God for gathering and strengthening the church so that the saints can minister (Acts 2:33).

They also needed power which would enable them to do the mission. In the Greek, the word for power is δύναμις *dunamis*, the root of the word dynamite. They needed the power of the Spirit to move them in the work. Jesus told us, there is going to be Someone who comes along side you to accomplish this mission, Who will in fact, do the mission through you (John 16). And before they were to go out on this mission, Jesus said to them:

> But you shall receive **power** when the Holy Spirit has come upon you; and you shall be **witnesses to Me** in Jerusalem, and in all Judea and Samaria, and to the end of the earth (Acts 1:8, emphasis added).

Jesus didn't say wait in Jerusalem until you are born again. Jesus didn't say wait in Jerusalem until you've been converted, or wait until you are united to the body of Christ universal, etc. Rather, Jesus said wait until you are clothed with power. Power for service. Power for extraordinary prophetic empowerment! And the

Holy Spirit in and through the Church began to turn the world upside down.

In the power of the Holy Spirit, mission impossible became mission unstoppable. On the Day of Pentecost, the disciples received spiritual gifts and power for service. Peter preached the gospel and 3,000 people became disciples (Acts 2:41). Now that's power!

Likewise, we are on the same mission and through the power of the Spirit, mission impossible becomes "mission unstoppable." Christ's promise is: I will always be with you and nothing can separate us (Mt 28:18-20; Jn 16:33). We are therefore called to go along with Jesus in His mission to transform the world with the gospel; nothing less than the renewing of humanity (2 Cor 5:7).

4. Proclamation – In the Book of Acts we observe the Church being moved along by the Holy Spirit in such a way that the Book is often rightly referred to as "the Acts of the Holy Spirit." Through the power of the Spirit, the church was carried as it were from the Upper Room to the very edge of the known world. And as the apostles declared the gospel, their message didn't consist of arguments for the existence of God, or easy messages carefully crafted so as not to wound anyone's conscience. The preaching of the early church consisted of "a simple recital of the great events connected with the historical appearance of Jesus Christ" and the testimony to His saving work in their lives.[3]

In John chapter 16, Jesus calls the Holy Spirit the "Helper." In the Greek, Helper is Παράκλητος *paracletos*. As Jesus told us, the Holy Spirit, as the

---

[3] Niebuhr, *The Meaning of Revelation*, 23.

Paraclete, took the place Christ's bodily presence. It is therefore by the indwelling Spirit that believers can experience Christ's presence. As Jesus teaches us, the Holy Spirit does His work in and through the Church to accomplish namely four principle tasks: (1) convict the world of sin (Jn 16:8); (2) guide believers into all truth (Jn 16:13); (3) declare things that are to come (Jn 16:13); and (4) glorify Christ (Jn 16:14).

By these means the Spirit works in and through the church to bring about the ordained plan of God (Eph 1:11). Jesus says the first thing the Holy Spirit does in a person's life is He convicts them of sin, showing men and women their desperate state. Then Jesus says there's three ways in which the Spirit's convicting work takes place: The Spirit convicts the world that sin is more grievous than they had ever imagined, that righteousness is more than they ever imagined, and that judgment is real, the Cross is real, and heaven and hell are real. It's the Holy Spirit that convicts people of all of these truths.

In John 16:12-15, Jesus describes the work that the Spirit will do "by, with, and through" the Church. In fact, the history of the Church has been the legacy of the Spirit regenerating, inspiring and guiding the Church to carry the gospel to the ends of the earth and to all the nations. By God's design, the mission of the Church involves nothing short of the building of a house (Eph 2:19-22).

God has moved in extraordinary ways in the history of the Church, but that doesn't mean that the Spirit's work is all but history. Let's not come to Acts chapter two with a mere academic interest in some distant, unrepeatable event. Regarding spiritual gifts, it's not that the gifts are no longer needed, in many cases, the gifts are no longer desired. The Church today needs power for service. Therefore, we need all the gifts to complete our mission. Until the task of world evangelization is completed, our duty is to pray for fresh seasons of the extraordinary outpouring of God's Spirit, to awaken us, empower us, and carry us forward until the mission is complete (Mt 28:18-20).

The point is: without the presence and power of the Holy Spirit the task of world evangelism or any evangelism is a mission impossible. We have our part to play and our part to play is dependent on the Holy Spirit's transcendent power. In other words, the Holy Spirit accomplishes the impossible mission through us.

As the Early Church proclaimed the gospel, they did so with the conviction that there was salvation found in no other Name than the Name of Jesus, and that as many as were appointed unto eternal life would believe (Acts 4:12; 13:48). Likewise, we must be ever mindful of God's sovereignty and His divine appointments. Often a pastor will spend more time concerned with precision in exegesis over biblical texts, which is of course very important. However, they can allow the concern for exegetical precision to blind them to those around them who haven't heard the message of the gospel. And so, when an opportunity presents itself, though you are running late, see the opportunity for what it is, a divine appointment. Be ready to take action and be obedient by sharing the gospel with everyone you come into contact with. Even when these opportunities don't go so well, the gospel has still done its work. And we cannot know what is going on in that person's life. A seed is sown. In the case of rejection, the gospel has still done its work (Acts 13:46).

As we go into the enemy's camp, Scripture is our offensive weapon. Scripture gives believers the tools necessary to harvest souls in evangelism. There are various techniques for sharing the gospel: The Roman Road, the Way of the Master, Evangelism Explosion, etc. The best technique is simply to share Jesus in your testimony with the Word of God. In this way, the person being witnessed to is being confronted with God's Word as it is living and active, sharper than any two-edged sword (Heb 4:12; cf. 2 Tim 3:16-17).

One of the reasons why many fail to witness is because when they have, it has ended in a heated disagreement. However, the results of an evangelical encounter aren't up to us. It's between them and God. We are simply being obedient to the gospel task. Even if you don't have the privilege to see someone respond the first time you share your faith, you have not failed, because you were obedient. It's not about success or failure, it's about obedience on our part. Results are not up to us. This fact should give us more confidence as we share our faith.

5. Provision – Something the Book of Acts also demonstrates for us is how we are to provide for the needs of new believers. In Acts chapter two, Peter preaches a message that ends up saving three thousand people. Then the rest of the chapter outlines how the apostles were obedient to the Great Commission. As Jesus commanded, "Go therefore and make disciples of all the nations, baptizing them in the name of the Father and of the Son and of the Holy Spirit, teaching them to observe all things that I have commanded you" (Mt 28:19-20). Those 3,000 who gladly received Peter's message were then baptized and brought into the community of faith. There they learned the apostle's doctrine, and as part of the messianic community, they enjoyed Christian fellowship, prayer and partook of the Lord's Supper (Acts 2:41-42).

As has been said, our shepherding care is our stewarding of those who belong to Jesus. The principle of provision therefore reminds us that as we tend Christ's sheep, we edifying them with God's Word and disciple them, helping them discover their gifts and step out to use them.

6. Persecution – Jesus said, you will be hated by everyone, and those who kill you, will do so thinking they offer God service (Jn 15:23; 16:2). In the Bible and the history of the Church, many of God's prophets, apostles and church leaders have been filled with the Spirit of God to convict the world of sin and draw people's heart in repentance and faith toward God. They were filled with power and were anointed to say and do amazing and miraculous things. But at the height of what the Spirit did through them, instead of national conversion or reformation, instead there was intense enmity directed at the offending message and the messenger.

A famous example is Elijah and his contest with the prophets of Baal. While all the false prophets could do is wear themselves out, God answered Elijah by fire, then answered his prayer for rain. Yet at the height of what the Spirit did thru Elijah, there was no national repentance and no conversion or reformation. And because of this, Elijah said he wanted to die. But God took him on the mountain and gave him a lesson. And the lesson was this: God can move in a mighty wind, He can move in a mighty earthquake or a blazing fire. But the most penetrating revelation of God to man is a still, small voice. The still small voice is God's chosen way of saving mankind.

Likewise, Jesus says: I am telling you this now so that when trouble comes your way on account of your witness your faith in me may not be shaken. This should be very encouraging for us. Often, we think, unless we have a big meeting with a good sound system, and the right lighting, and just the right musicians and the right preachers and teachers then it will not produce great results. The point is: God may not be working as we expect Him to, but He is working all the same. And He is working in spite of trouble, against impossible odds, and the most hardened heart.

This is what you do with soldiers you intend to send into harm's way. You tell them, "Look, this isn't going to be a picnic. It's combat." They say, to be forewarned is to be forearmed. Jesus says, count on having conflict.

7. Perseverance – In the Bible, God caricatures His bride, the Church, as a woman in labor giving birth to all of His people. Isn't that amazing! In fact, this topic underscores many central texts of Scriptures, such as: Genesis 3, Isaiah 26, John 16, Romans 8, and Revelation 12. In these texts, there is a running theme: There is a woman, an adversary, the woman's sorrow and pain to bring forth birth, and deliverance through judgment. In John 16:20-21, Jesus gives us a parabolic expression which incorporates these main elements of thought. Jesus says:

> 20 Most assuredly, I say to you that you will weep and lament, but the world will rejoice; and you will be sorrowful, but your sorrow will be turned into joy.
> 21 A woman, when she is in labor, has sorrow because her hour has come; but as soon as she has

> given birth to the child, she no longer remembers the anguish, for joy that a human being has been born into the world.

One of the ways the Bible pictures God's people is that of a barren woman wearied by her inability to give birth to her promised spiritual children. Though she is experiencing the pangs of childbirth, she can't deliver.

Something this teaches us is the church has never saved anyone. We can't give any one new birth, only the Holy Spirit can. What Jesus teaches us in John 16: 20-21 is: While I'm away, this interadvent period between My first coming and Second Coming, my messianic community will be like a woman in labor. That is, the church will be like a woman in the pangs of labor to give birth to all of God's people. And that which is brought forth during this interadvent period is the new birth of regenerated humanity.

In other words, the mission is possible not because we have dedicated followers. There are world systems and religions that have droves of fanatics that are willing to suffer and die for what they believe. So do the cults. The Church, however, must rely on the Spirit's presence and power to complete the Great Commission. This is the principle of perseverance.

We don't need to rely on money, political power or influence, we have the Spirit. We can count on the Helper, the Paraclete to be with us. In this world, we will continue to suffer until all of God elect come in (2 Tim 2:10). As Paul declares: "For this light and momentary affliction is working for us a far more exceeding and eternal weight of glory" (2 Cor 4:17). In other words, our labor and pain to gather in God's elect is light and momentary, and through the power of the

Spirit, we'll gather in all God's people, and that's for God's glory; an eternal weight of glory. God, who ordained the salvation of His elect, also ordained that they would be saved through the preaching of the gospel.

The principle of perseverance is, we can count on conquest despite the appearance of defeat (Jn 16: 31-33). Jesus said, "Indeed the hour is coming, yes, has now come, that you will be scattered, each to his own, and will leave Me alone." This is what immediately happened. The Shepherd was struck and the sheep were shattered, and they all denied ever knowing Jesus, and He went to the cross and suffered and died. All looked lost. It looked like complete defeat. But Christ conquered through defeat. He conquered through the cross.

Likewise, Jesus is telling us, My church will conquer though it looks defeated. In Jn 16:20, Jesus says: "you will weep and lament, but the world will rejoice; and you will be sorrowful, but your sorrow will be turned into joy." A question we may ask is: Why does the church have to suffer? And the short answer is: God delays His final judgment until the full number of His people are saved: "The Lord knows those who are His" (2 Tim 2:19).

There is a number known only to God. There is a remnant chosen by grace. Moreover, those known by God and called by God come to Christ and to His church. And this delaying of God's final judgment is going to cause us suffering. The reason why Jesus is telling His disciples this is because the nature of His kingdom will be very different than what they've imagined. It will look pathetic, but it's powerful.

Suffering occurs because the judgment is delayed until the full number of God's people come in. Evangelical missionaries entered Cambodia in the 1920s. By the time they were expelled in 1965 there were about 600 believers. Then civil war came and between 1965 and 1975 during the civil war the Christian population soared to an estimated 90,000. It was an amazing work of God. But when the Khmer Rouge took control and Pol Pot unleashed his fury on the nation, most of these Christians died or fled the country. In all, about 30 % percent of the Cambodian people and 90% of the Cambodian Church were wiped out. And yet it was like grains of seed falling into the Cambodian soil.

Suffering also affords the church an opportunity to testify. In Cambodia, this occurred in a powerful way. Pol Pot's communist forces surrounded and laid siege to the capital of Phnom Penh. In the midst of the chaos, Cambodian Christians spread out all over the city preaching the gospel to crowds, winning souls and rescuing them from the jaws of hell. Pol Pot' reign of terror is now gone but the Church lives on. The Church in Cambodia looked pathetic, but it was powerful.

Christ's promise is: I will always be with you and nothing can separate us (Mt 28:20). This is the security that a perfect atonement secures. This is why Jesus teaches us not to be fooled by appearances. Jesus said: "These things I have spoken to you, that in Me you may have peace. In the world you will have tribulation; but be of good cheer, I have overcome the world" (Jn 16:33). Understanding this verse is one of the great keys to living the Christian life.

The Bible teaches us that Jesus Christ is reigning now and is in the process of putting all His enemies under His feet. Moreover, Jesus' words: "I have overcome the world" or I have conquered the world in is in the Greek perfect tense. The unique thing about the perfect tense is that it emphasizes the present and ongoing result of a completed action. The point is this: All things are declared subject to Christ already but somethings remain to be brought into subjection. What is Jesus is the process of doing now? He is in the process of subjecting all things under His feet.

In other words, Christ has conquered the world and is conquering the world (Jn 16:33). And the amazing thing is, that's how God talks about His church. In the Epistle of First John, the apostle John applies this to the church and says: "I write to you, because you have overcome the wicked one" (1 Jn 2:13). This truth motivated a stanza in Luther's hymn *A Mighty Fortress is Our God*: "Though this world with devils filled should threaten to undo us, we will not fear for God hath willed His truth to triumph through us."

Personal Evangelism

As pastors, our role is to lead the Church in evangelism and disciple-making. One way we can do that is encourage our people toward personal evangelism. It is said that more than three quarters of all new believers come to Christ through a friend or acquaintance. This number far exceeds those who come to Christ through an evangelical event.[4] This fact reminds us that Christ's command to make disciples by

---

[4] William Fay and Linda Evans Shepherd, *Share Jesus Without Fear* (Nashville, TN: B&H, 1999), 12.

evangelizing others is not merely for ordained ministers but for every believer (Mt 28:18-20). What is more often the most debilitating issue in evangelism is fear. But fear should never inhibit us from sharing the good news (1 Pet 3:15). Success in evangelism is defined as sharing your faith and living your life for Jesus Christ.

Ultimately, whether a person comes to faith in Christ or not is not up to us but rather upon God who shows mercy. God is sovereign in the salvation of sinners, and we could very well be yet another witness in a perhaps a long line of witnesses giving a particular person the gospel (Jn 6:44). Besides, the mixed reaction of the Pentecost crowd should remind us that the "miraculous is not self-authenticating, nor does it inevitably and uniformly convince."[5] The challenge is therefore to forego excuses and simply be faithful by sharing your faith and living your life for Jesus Christ. In the last analysis, when people reject the good news, they are rejecting God, not us, the messenger. And so, when we share our faith, we can't fail because the results belong to God.

Looking again at the principle of prayer, we must pray that God would move upon the lost. The farmer breaks upon the ground and sows the seed but the results are of the Lord. Pray that the Lord will speak to the lost through testimony. In the last analysis, success in evangelism is sharing your faith and living your life for Jesus Christ. We can and should do this without fear. My prayer is that the Lord will stir our hearts and gives us a heart as big as His for the lost. My prayer is

---

[5] Tremper Longman III and David E. Garland, *Expositor's Bible Commentary. Volume 10. Luke-Acts* (Grand Rapids: Zondervan, 2007).

that we will be those who talk to the lost, rather than those who merely talk about the lost.

The mission of the Paraclete will continue while the world lasts. As we seek to fulfill the mission the Holy Spirit is doing through us, we need what every church needs: A fresh empowering in ministry, greater effectiveness in prayer and Bible study, and joy in worship. This is what the church calls revival, which is the renewal and reawakening of the church from within. We need a fresh empowering for ministry, a significant step in Christian growth. Following the pattern of the Book of Acts, we need to be filled again and again and again with the Holy Spirit. Through the Spirit's presence and power, mission impossible is mission unstoppable.

Chapter Fourteen: Preaching and Teaching

"Be diligent to present yourself approved to God, a worker who does not need to be ashamed, rightly dividing the word of truth." – 2 Timothy 2:15

Preaching and teaching are words we use a lot but nobody is quite sure what the difference between them is. What is the difference? Is it that preaching is fiery and teaching is dry? Is it that preaching aims at the heart, and teaching at the head? There's a grain of truth here but rather I think the answer is rests in the meanings of the words themselves. Preaching in the Greek is κηρύσσω *kerusso* and means "to herald." In the ancient world, a herald rode into town to deliver significant news. On the other hand, teaching, in the Greek διδάσκω *didasko* means "to instruct." This to me seems to be the difference.

Preaching is heralding and proclaiming news to people – the gospel – especially (but not exclusively) to those who haven't heard it before. Teaching is explaining things about the gospel that people don't understand, and instructing them on how to live in light of it. The most helpful illustration of this comes from John Piper. He pictures a herald riding into town, shouting from high atop his horse, "Hear ye! Hear ye! The Emperor has declared an amnesty to all slaves!" That, Piper says, is preaching: proclaiming good news, announcing something that has happened, that completely changes the situation of the listeners. But he then imagines people approaching the herald with questions. What does amnesty mean? When does this announcement take effect? Does that mean I can leave my slave master now? Will compensation be paid to masters? And so on.

At that point, you have to start teaching: explaining the implications of the news, helping people with concepts and ideas they don't understand, and telling people what they need to do in response, given their various situations. In other words, the difference between preaching and teaching is not shouting versus whispering, or revealing versus informing. It's essentially the difference between heralding and explaining.

Both preaching and teaching are to occupy the time of God's man. Preaching and teaching is truth mediated through personality; a sermon includes both. Preaching and teaching is not mere entertainment, nor a mere display of, nor merely the seven steps to better parenting, or a better marriage, or becoming a better you, etc. Preaching and teaching must also be theological but not merely a lecture on theology, nor merely a class. In fact, preaching is not preaching if it is watered down to make people more comfortable. By God' design it's to be a proclamation of the truth of God as mediated through personality, so that "whoever speaks, as one who speaks oracles of God" (1 Pet 4:11).

Here are some helpful gems I've learned preaching. Preaching is theology from a man who is on fire! A preacher should crave the unction of the Holy Ghost so as to preach as he has never preached before, as a dying man to dying men! It's not difficult for a preacher to distinguish between mere pulpit eloquence and spiritual unction. The first will lift him up; the second will humble him in awe.

As has been said, the sermon must be theological and not merely a lecture on theology, nor merely a class. We are called to preach the gospel not about it. The sermon should be derived from the Scripture and always be textual. A sermon is comparative to a symphony. It mustn't deal with any text in isolation, the greatest care should be made to keep the text within its context.

Moreover, because good teaching requires driving home biblical truth, repetition in a sermon is good. The sermon should always be expositional. Additionally, the sermon should be derived from the whole counsel of God and include doctrinal content. The sheep need food. As Martyn Lloyd-Jones put it, "Feed the sheep; don't entertain the goats." The sermon is no mere essay. It's not merely a display of the preacher's knowledge, as William Perkins put it "The preaching of the Word is the testimony of God, not human wisdom."

According to Perkins, there are four interrogative questions we may ask of any particular scripture passage:

1. What does this particular scripture teach?
2. How does this apply to us today?
3. What are we to do in response?
4. How does scripture teach us to do it?

As we approach Scripture for the purposes of exposition, we should not interpret any verse in the light of our experiences, but we should examine our experiences in the light of the teaching of the scriptures.[111]

True preaching is centered squarely on the cross. The cross of Christ is so central to the gospel that the

---

[111] Martyn Lloyd-Jones, Joy Unspeakable, 17.

apostle Paul referred to it as the word or message of the cross. The preaching of the cross is "foolish ness to those who are perishing, but to us who are being saved it is the power of God" (1 Cor 1:18). The cross is so central that when the apostle Paul came to Corinth, a center for pagan thought, he didn't engage them along philosophical lines but said that he "determined not to know anything among you except Jesus Christ and him crucified" (1 Cor 2:2).

Ralph Turnbull writes, "The preaching which calls for no sacrifice, no cross or resurrection, no kingdom demands, will entertain and amuse some bit it will not secure disciples."[112]

And lastly, you should have a main thrust in the sermon and arrive at a particular doctrine(s). You should be careful to consider the relevance of it and demonstrate its importance. If possible, following Perkins, indicate the main theme and its various divisions in the introduction: (1) explain the context; (2) examine important words; and (3) extrapolate (draw out) the lesson(s) – **E3**. Above all, faithful preaching of the gospel is Christ centered, structured by Scripture, and urgent.

What the Church of all generations desperately needs is biblically sound Christ-centered preaching. "God has spoken! But what has He said?"[113] This is the basic need of biblical interpretation. There have been countless errors in the Church. Many have treated Scripture as if it were a wax nose, fashioning it according to their pleasure.

---

[112] Turnbull, The Preacher's Heritage, Task, and Resources, 76.

[113] Bernard Ramm, *Protestant Biblical Interpretation* (Grand Rapids: Baker, 1970) 2.

Preaching the Word is prophesying (forthtelling) in the name and on behalf of Christ. Through preaching, those who hear are called into the state of grace, and preserved in it. The Preacher must break up the fallow ground. According to the Puritan William Perkins, there are four axioms of preaching:

First, there is the primacy of the intellect. "Everyman's first duty in relation to the Word of God is to understand it; and every preacher's first duty is to explain it." Likewise, Perkins spoke of three aims to every sermon: (1) humble the sinner; (2) exalt the Savior; and (3) promote holiness. Second, a belief in the supreme importance of preaching. "Nothing honors God more than the faithful declaration and obedient hearing of his truth." [114] Third, a belief in the life-giving power of the Holy Scripture. "Better not preach at all than preach beyond the Bible." Fourth, a belief in the Sovereignty of the Holy Spirit. "Man's task is simply to be faithful in teaching the Word; it is God's work to convince of its truth and write it on the heart."

A tool of the *Navigators* I have used over the years that is very helpful for Bible study and considering the overall thrust of a passage is the acronym **SPECK**:

S – Sin to avoid (Does the passage address any particular sin to avoid?).
P – Promise to keep (Does the passage address any of God's promises?).
E – Example to follow (Is there an example to follow in The passage?).
C – Command to obey (Are there any commands?).
K – Knowledge to glean (What particular truths are There to know?).

---

[114] Ibid.

Chapter Fifteen: Counseling

"Shepherding is synonymous with pastoral care."
– Alistair Begg

Counseling is to bring comfort, change and hope by God's Spirit and Word. Counseling is meeting the needs of hurting people with God's truth. A counselor offers who he is in Christ.[1] Counseling looks to the cause of a problem and seeks to uproot it. It seeks to lift up the downcast. To bring good news (Is 52:7). Through counseling, God comforts those who mourn, brings beauty for ashes, and the oil of joy for mourning, and the garment of praise for the spirit of heaviness (Is 61:3). The goal in counseling is to bring all life under the Lordship of Christ, to live life as God wills it (Jn 14:15; Gal 5:6).

The Christian's approach to counseling should always begin from the tenet *Sola Scriptura* as Scripture is the only divinely authoritative and infallible source for the rule of life (2 Tim 3:16). Everything begins with the truth revealed to us in the Word of God. Secular and biblical theories begin from different (at most times antithetical) starting points. To the secular worldview, man is the measure, and therefore solutions are sought within man in a reliance to his resources; the goal being self-actualizing so as to "develop your full potential and live your best life now."[2]

---

[1] Rupp, OPT501, Introduction to Counseling.

[2] Additionally, over against Arminianism, Reformed theology frames biblical counseling with the correct view of man – he is dead, defiled, and damned and will remain so unless Christ in His grace saves him.

Sola Scriptura keeps Christ's preeminence in focus and seeks to expose the deeper internal problems of sin and guilt, with the stated goal of seeking God's glory in all things (1 Cor 10:31). Sola Scriptura reminds the Christian counselor that when secular research conflicts with Scripture, it must be rejected.[1] Tim Keller observes,

Psychology and biblical theology deal with different dimensions of human life, use different methods of study, ask different questions, and look at two different things. The Bible looks at the human spirit and relationship to God. Psychology looks at how the human brain functions, how people adapt and react to natural and social environments.[2]

In light of what has been said about secular and biblical counseling, the biggest differences are the starting off points and purposes. However, for the Christian counselor everything begins with the inerrant Word of God; the goal, achieving peace with God by living life God's way in the strength only He can provide. How then are we to view secular theories? Whereas the goal of secular counseling must be rejected, however, because of God's common grace, many secular theories provide useful insights when they are filtered through the grid of Scripture. Thus, while the Bible is sufficient for all our needs, secular theories may help Christian counselors diagnose certain problems.

We may therefore employ some secular theories with the understanding that "all truth is God's truth."[3]

[1] For example, a commonly held view in psychology today is that homosexuality is due to biological factors (the so-called gay gene).

[2] Keller, *Four Models of Counseling in Pastoral Ministry*, 2.

[3] Carter & Narramore, *The Integration of Psychology and Theology*, 22.

However, we must take them with a grain of salt (Mt 5:13) as Jay Adams has rightly noted, "Psychotherapy has become little more than a search through one's past for others on whom to place the blame."[4] This has warrant, as the secular worldview invariably ends up blaming a person's problems on certain external factors (parents, abuse, etc.) while the real problems, the internal ones (sin, guilt, strongholds, etc.) are not addressed, with the result being the person counseled is never set free from their burden. Given secular counseling's humanistic approach, the Christian counselor must be ever judicious in its use.

For example, Freud may help mine into one's iceberg past. And while we should avoid his tendency for blaming all our problems on others, we may readily employ some of his techniques to better understand unconscious motives to bring them under the Lordship of Christ (Jn 14:15). We can also find that Horney's theory on neurotic tendencies (*Our Inner Conflicts*) can help us understand how neurosis can take root in childhood. Furthermore, concepts like 'transference,' 'operant conditioning,' and 'cognitive-dissonance' may help us understand why people do some of the things they do.

Further, much can be found of practical value in Adler's 'birth order' or the idea that "what we think we lack determines what we will become in life" (inferiority complex).[5] Because of common grace, secular theories may not take the counselor where he needs to go, but they may point him in the right direction. The point being made here is where the

---

[4] Adams, *Competent to Counsel*, xvii.
[5] Butler-Bowden, 50 Psychological Classics, 14.

theories of Freud, Rogers or Adler do not conflict with God's Word, they should be considered for use by the Christian counselor in order to help others. This presents a holistic approach to Christian counseling.

Beginning from *Sola Scriptura*, counseling brings comfort, change and hope by God's Spirit and Word. Counseling confronts sin in our lives. Sin is an affront to God and unconfessed sin regardless of diagnosis brings wrath. Further, people have particular needs which ultimately can only be met in Christ alone. Therefore, a Christian counselor's approach should be three-pronged: First, he is to be guided and directed by God the Holy Spirit. Second, as formulated by Adams, he should emphasize a direct confrontation with sin. Third, as formulated by Crabb, the counselor should emphasize dealing with needs of significance and security.

Principles of Biblical Counseling

With an understanding of this approach, we need to discuss the practical aspects of biblical counseling. A Christian counselor is a helper who seeks to bring the person and the problem under the power and presence of God. The following principles in the acronym **HELPER** follow a linear progression, and are an attempt to do just that:

H – Holy Spirit.
E – Empathy (positive).
L – Listening (active).
P – Proposed goals.
E – Execution.
R – Referral as necessary.

Holy Spirit: The first principle in biblical counseling reminds us of our total reliance on the mind of God for any hope of deliverance (Jn 14:26). Seeking the presence and power of God, the counselor relies on the leading, guidance and direction of the third Person of the Trinity (1 Jn 2:1).
Counseling is to begin and end with prayer. Additionally, the counselor should be expectant and ever desirous of the leading of the Holy Spirit to guide and direct all discussion – the foremost approach in all counseling (Jn 16:12-15; 2 Tim 3:16).

Empathy: the second principle, is helpful throughout the entire counseling process. Empathy means "communicating initial basic understanding of what the client is feeling and of the experiences and behaviors underlying these feelings."[6] The goal is to create a positive environment which facilitates the Spirit's work. The approach behind this principle is to uncover sin and the problems associated it. The counselor's desire is that he be used by God as an instrument of bringing comfort, change and hope by God's Spirit and Word.

The third principle: **Listening**, is to be active with eye contact with the goal of minimizing nonverbal behavior; as these can be distracting and counterproductive to counseling. While implementing the first three principles, an exploration should be underway to uncover the root cause of the problem (the reason why the person is getting counseled). This principle highlights a need to be receptive to the Spirit and the Word to find a solution to the presented problem. Underscoring this principle is the approach

[6] Egan, *The Skilled Helper*, 87.

which seeks uncovering issues involving significance and security. Ultimately, a person may not feel worthy or accepted, but they are responsible to believe God's Word, because one's critical need for security and significance are found in Christ alone.[7]

The fourth principle is: **Proposed goals**. Here a decision should be reached as to what steps will be taken to fix the problem. Here an attempt is made to challenge a person's understanding of what is troubling them. It may involve repentance for sin, asking forgiveness or forgiving others. The goal is to envision an endstate which will free the person from guilt and sin and a possible reliance on neurotic tendencies. Sin must be owned and dealt with. The gospel is to be always in focus.

The fifth principle: **Execution**, seeks to implement the proposed goals. Here a plan is set in motion. The counselor at this stage navigates the action, avoiding potential obstacles. These obstacles may include: resistance from the client, getting bogged down, a client's losing of motivation, and quitting altogether. The counselor, who should be keen to all guidance and direction of the Holy Spirit, seeks to bring God's presence and power along the way, especially at times where things seem to stall and become ineffective. Above all, the counselor should seek to instill hope in the healing power of the gospel.

The sixth and last principle is **Referral as necessary**. The counselor should determine with the guidance and direction of the Holy Spirit if a problem is a sin or chemical imbalance issue. And if the later he may have to supplement his counsel with a referral for

---

[7] Crabb, *Inside Out*, 80-88.

psychiatric medication. This last principle reminds counselors that they have limitations. A Christian counselor can probably help people with neuroses, and depression, but only at a certain level as persons with psychosis in reality will need medication and hospitalization in addition to biblical counsel.

Pitfalls of Counseling

Counseling is to be for the glory of God and the good of His people. As counselors our motives need to be pure. Counselors are to be motivated and actuated by the love of Christ and not the flesh (2 Cor 5:14). The nurturing and sanctification of the saints is God's concern and the devil's target. There are several pitfalls a Christian counselor should avoid. They relate directly to the three approaches in counseling which were: (1) God the Spirit directs and guides; (2) sin is exposed; and (3) an emphasis needs to be placed on significance and security.

There are four main pitfalls. These encompass the variety of mistakes a counselor can make or problem issues he may fail to detect and eliminate. Pitfalls may be remembered with the acronym **S4**: Scripture, Sin, Significance, and Security.

The first pitfall is neglecting Scripture. The counselor is to be guided and directed by God the Holy Spirit and must remember he is not God. *Sola Scriptura* reminds him that he should never allow his own opinions to outweigh that of Scripture. This is the chief line of demarcation between secular and Christian counseling. Counseling cannot take God's place. His almighty Word is the healing and delivering instrument. Additionally, this pitfall reminds counselors not to neglect themselves and their families.

The second pitfall is emphasizing the symptom and missing the cause. Christian counseling seeks to bring comfort to those who mourn but also to expose sin and bring one's life and problems under Christ's Lordship (Lk 6:46).[8] At this point the counselor should be mindful if the problem is that of sin or chemical imbalance. In other words, although a person suffering from bipolar is a sinner and sins, barring God's miraculous deliverance, their problem is their mental illness, and will require medication in addition to your counsel.

The third pitfall deals with one's need of significance. In Christian counseling, the emphasis should always be on God and His Word. A counselor should avoid: the idea that his counsel is discipleship; and doing too much for the client. There's only so much a counselor can do, as he has limited time and energy. We can't do everything for those we counsel. Backus observes, "It's good to be aware of your limits."[9]

The fourth and last major pitfall is involves security. This reminds the counselor that there must be safe guards in place that protect both the counselor and the counselee. A neglect of safeguards can lead to allegations on the one hand, and a potentially dangerous situation on the other. To begin with, if the counselor is a man providing help to a woman, he should be accompanied by another woman with some counseling training if possible. At the same time this protects all parties involved from any hearsay and

---

[8] Christian counseling in this sense may be looked at as the process of sanctification in the life of the believer.

[9] Backus, *Telling the Truth to Troubled People*, 49-50.

avoids the appearance of evil (1 Thess 5:22). On the other hand, a counselor's unwillingness to refer a client with problems beyond his degree of effectiveness can lead to dangerous life-threatening situations. On this and all levels, balance is imperative in counseling.

The Role of the Church in Counseling

According to the Word of God, caring for souls – sustaining sufferers and transforming sinners – is a component of the total ministry of the church.[10] Every minister is enabled and expected by the Lord to counsel someone at some point.[11] Counseling begins in the church with the goal of bringing all life under the Lordship of Christ (Col 1:18). Pastors help those in their congregation who are struggling with their faith, depression, marital problems, alcoholism, drug abuse, bulimia, sexual deviation, etc. God's house is a house of prayer and supplication. And the Almighty God knows our deepest needs and provides for them in the wisest ways (Is 65:24). In order to encourage hurting people, pastors can enlist the help of their congregations. A good pastoral approach is to: (1) educate the congregation in the basics of biblical counseling; and (2) motivate members to do counseling.[12]

Practically, this involves a trained congregant sitting in on a counseling session to observe and work alongside the counselor. By training a congregation in biblical counseling, a pastor can assemble a team of skilled helpers whom God can employ in and out of

---

[10] McMinn and Phillips, *Care for the Soul: Exploring the Intersection of Psychology & Theology*, 54.
[11] Adams, *Shepherding God's Flock*, 174.
[12] Adams, *Shepherding God's Flock*, 199.

therapy sessions (Rom 15:14; Gal 6:1; James 4:2-3). Many people feel unwelcomed in church either because of their own feelings of inadequacy and neurosis or sense of a zero fault mentality that may permeate. The point here is the church is for hurting people. It's a sort of hospital for people who don't have all the answers and resources – Christians.

In light of this, what should be a congregational approach to persons suffering with personality disorders, or schizophrenia and bipolar? A pastor should cultivate an environment to minister to these groups to provide a healing community. In saying this, some people may be very 'taxing' on the congregation. It will require the congregation to explore fully and in the deepest sense what Paul really means in 1 Corinthians 13 and to visit those who are in pain with the goal of bringing them the love of Christ Who is with them though the pain may remain.

A Christian's view of counseling should ever be one that envisions God's Word and Spirit ministering through the instrumentality of a humble believer with the goal bringing comfort, change and hope. In biblical counseling, the counselor and one counseled both expect and greatly desire the power and presence of the risen Christ to guide and direct the discussion to bring about deliverance. For whereas psychology says 'pull yourself up,' Christian counseling says 'seek God's counsel' (1 Kgs 22:5; Ps 42:5, 11; Is 8:19; Mt 16:33).

Chapter Sixteen: Protecting the Flock

"Though the terror upon our adversary would be greater if we all were more uniform, we follow the same colors. And though not clothed alike, and differing in things less significant, against the common enemy, Christians march as soldiers all under the same Captain." – Jeremiah Burroughs

In this chapter we return to where we left off in chapter two in our discussion of the pastor as Christ's undershepherd, particularly his responsibility to protect the flock with nurturing care.

Ten years ago, an American pastor by the name of Tim Laniak was visiting a friend in Jordan with his son. The pastor's friend was an Arab shepherd. The shepherd said to Tim, "My sons don't have the heart for this work so I can't trust them with the family business. Tim, you have the heart for it, and so does your 13-year-old son." And then he said, "You tell your son I'll give him 200 sheep, a wife and a good Jordanian education. Ask him to think about it and give me an answer tomorrow. Tim's son politely declined the offer. By that experience Tim learned how much his Bedouin friend valued a shepherd's heart.

After centuries of failed leadership in ancient Israel, God promised His people through the prophet Jeremiah that He would give them shepherds after His own heart. In Jeremiah's day, God watched the community's leaders, and like Tim's friend, didn't think they couldn't be trusted with the family business because they didn't have the Owner's heart. In fact, God condemned these false shepherds through the prophet Ezekiel. He said in Ezek 34:2-4:

> Woe to the shepherds of Israel who have been feeding yourselves! Should not shepherds feed the sheep? 3 You eat the fat, you clothe yourselves with the wool, you slaughter the fat ones, but you do not feed the sheep. 4 The weak you have not strengthened, the sick you have not healed, the injured you have not bound up, the strayed you have not brought back, the lost you have not sought, and with force and harshness you have ruled them.

Then Ezekiel prophesied that God Himself would come to shepherd them. And then centuries later, a voice was heard which said "I am the good shepherd. The good shepherd lays down his life for the sheep" (Jn 10:11).

It is God's intent to fully shape your calling, and identity as a pastor with this shepherd image. Jesus called a group of unremarkable men to serve with Him and He sent them out as spiritual shepherds of "the lost sheep of Israel." The mission of the apostles was in fact an extension of Jesus' pastoral mission.

Likewise, Christ continues to shepherd His sheep through His undershepherds. Christ calls His own sheep by name and places them in a particular congregation and calls on His undershepherds to provide them with shepherding care. This care involves oversight and patience, bearing up with their faults, and essentially amounts to watching and warning. Pastors are called to protect Christ's sheep from: (1) False teachers (Acts 20:28); (2) false doctrine (Acts 20:30); and (3) false practice (Acts 20:31).

It goes without saying, it is the pastor's responsibility to address dangerous elements in the congregation, both physical and spiritual. Sin is not to be tolerated within a congregation. If it goes unchecked, God will hold that whole church body accountable (Heb 13:17; Rev 2:22). By God's intent, as believers submit to the authority of the church, it is an expression of their submission to God (Ps 133; Rom 13:1). Essentially, protecting the flock under your care amounts to watching and warning with the Shepherd's heart and is a call to the congregation to submit to the godly leadership of the pastor.

Watch – In the Book of Hebrews, the apostle exhorts us to "Remember those who rule over you," and "obey those who rule over you, and be submissive, for they *watch out* for your souls, as those who must give account" (Heb 13:7, 17, emphasis added). A pastor is called to protect the flock from pernicious elements. In Acts 20, the Apostle Paul urges the Ephesian elders to be on the lookout for false teachers. He says: "For I know this, that after my departure savage wolves will come in among you, not sparing the flock" (Acts 20:29).

False teachers can worm their way into people's homes by way of radio, television and books. Paul says, even from their own congregations, false teachers would arise and speak "perverse things" and draw people away (Acts 20:30-31). Doctrinal purity is essential to the health of any congregation. However, it is essential for a pastor not to be a "mote" hunter. Every pastor wants the congregation to be on the same page doctrinally that he is. But that is rarely the case. Augustine's axiom is useful as we consider doctrinal purity: "In essentials unity, in non-essentials liberty, and in all things charity." This reminds us that in order to maintain the unity of the Spirit in the bond of peace we should "keep the main thing, the main thing." Doctrine matters. Christians share "one Lord, one faith, one baptism, and one God and Father of all" (Eph 4:5-6).

If Christians can share the fundamental tenets of the Christian faith, such as those that are encapsulated in the Apostle's and Nicene creeds, the essentials, then they can share the common faith. However, once there is doctrinal apostasy, moral and ethical decline are an absolute certainty. This occurs when people turn away from the authority of the Scriptures. Regarding doctrine, overemphasizing doctrinal purity can lead to a lack of concern for the outside world (Rev 2:2-4) but deemphasizing doctrinal purity can lead to an over identification with the world (Rev 2:20).

Warn – In Ephesians 5:21, the Apostle Paul instructs Christians to "submit to one another in the fear of the Lord," as we "esteem others better than ourselves" (Phil 2:3). Likewise, the Apostle Peter exhorts younger people to "submit to their elders," and for everyone to "be submissive to one another, and be clothed with humility" (1 Pet 5:5).

It is the responsibility of the elders and deacons to address issues of sin in the church. That is why an elder is called an over-seer. This touches on discipline as one of the marks of a gospel church, and we must bear in mind its purpose – the restoration of a sinning brother. John MacArthur skillfully frames the parameters by observing, "The goal of church discipline is not to throw people out, embarrass them, be self-righteous, play God, or exercise authority and power in some unbiblical manner. The purpose of discipline is to bring people back into pure fellowship with God and others in the assembly."[1]

In Matthew 16:19, Jesus Christ entrusted His authority to "bind and loose" with Peter, the rest of the apostles, and the entire church (confer Mt 16:19 with Mt 18:18-20; 1 Cor 5:1-5; 1 Cor 5:12-13; 2 Cor 2:6-8; 1 Tim 1:20). Then in Matthew 18, Jesus teaches us how to act when a brother or sister has wandered from the Shepherd and the fold. Matthew 18:15-17 is the central governing passage for church discipline.

Jesus teaches us, "Moreover if your brother sins against you, go and tell him his fault between you and him alone. If he hears you, *you have gained your brother*. "But if he will not hear, take with you one or two more, that 'by the mouth of two or three witnesses every word may be established.' And if he refuses to hear them, tell it to the church. But if he refuses even to hear the church, let him be to you like a heathen and a tax collector" (Mt 18:16-17, emphasis added).

There are essentially two ways someone may sin, directly, such as against others personally, or indirectly, bringing reproach on the assembly. Both require of us to forgive as long as the person repents (Mt 18:22). In the context of Matthew 18:15, the word "gained," as in "you have gained your brother" is telling. The Greek word *kerdaino* refers to acquiring wealth, revealing the treasure we have recovered, our brother. James 5:19-20 teaches us, "Brethren, if anyone among you wanders from the truth, and someone turns him back, let him know that he who turns a sinner from the error of his way will save a soul from death and cover a multitude of sins."

---

[1] MacArthur, *The Master's Plan for the Church*, 267.

The watching and warning of others is part of a pastor's role. As imperfect as this may be, it is an extension of Jesus' pastoral mission. All of which is to be undergirded by Christ's humility and compassion for others. As Paul instructs us in Galatians 6:1, as we watch and warn for the purposes of restoring erring brothers, we are to do so "in a spirit of gentleness, considering yourself lest you also be tempted." As we watch and warn, everything is to be done with the Shepherd's heart, with sensitivity, the minimal amount of publicity, and the recovery of the sinning believer as the goal.

Regarding the recovery of an erring brother, there are mainly two things which are occurring: God is afflicting the sinning brother in some way (by way of his troubled conscience and perhaps temporal judgments), and the church is providing a voice (in love) to how God disapproves of the erring brother's sin. And in this way, the erring brother, detecting this transformative work of God, receives this corrective love, grows in grace and in the knowledge of God, by receiving God's correction from others (Pro 27:6). The whole experience can prove difficult, but if we love them, we'll do it. It's as D.A. Carson puts it, "if it is hard to accept a rebuke, even a private one, it is harder still to administer one in loving humility." [2]

Jesus teaches us how to act when a brother or sister has wandered from the fold of God. Every man that experiences the saving power of God should be open to God's fatherly disciplines when it comes at the hands of those he shares fellowship with. Thus, when the secrets of the wise man's heart is made manifest to his

---

[2] D.A. Carson, Matthew, 402.

brethren, it will result in repentance and renewed fellowship (1 Cor 14:25; Heb 4:11-13).

I have always been struck by the poetic polarity in Proverbs 9:8, Do not correct a scoffer, lest he hate you; rebuke a wise man, and he will love you. Though loving correction is offered to the wicked, they reject the overture, and despise you (Lk 14:15-24). Even something like, "please don't allow your child to bring their cellphone to children's church, it's distracting to others." If wisdom is rejected this will not be acquiesced to; Love's Labor's Lost. Even if grace is shown to the wicked, they will not learn righteousness, they will fail the test of discipleship because they cannot accept God's discipline by the hand of His people (Is 26:10). It is for this reason we must distance ourselves from holding on to bitterness. If we cannot endure God's Fatherly chastisements, then we demonstrate to all our sham religion.

On the contrary, "rebuke" a wise man, and he will love you. And verse 9 adds, "Give instruction to a wise man, and he will be still wiser; teach a just man, and he will increase in learning." The man who accepts the rebuke of wisdom shows himself to be wise. The man who loves the Lord, delights in His discipline, and can say along with David, Let the bones You have broken rejoice" (Ps 51:8). For God's discipline "yields the peaceable fruit of righteousness to those who have been trained by it" (Heb 12:11).

As a congregation, Christians are called to be submissive to each other: younger people to the older men in the church (1 Pet 5:5), women to their husbands (1 Pet 3:1), younger women to older women (Tit 2:3-4), and children to their parents and those older (Eph 6:1-3). And all Christians, regardless of age, should put on humility as a garment. These are the basic qualities of a sound church (Tit 2:1-10). It is in this atmosphere of mutual submission to Christ and others that discipleship becomes a reality.

But what about judging? Aren't Christians to avoid that sort of thing? Jesus told us to "judge not lest we be judged," but likewise He said, "Do not give what is holy to the dogs; nor cast your pearls before swine, lest they trample them under their feet, and turn and tear you in pieces (Mt 7:1, 6). So, what would Christ have us do? As Lloyd-Jones observes, "Merely to look at the word 'judge' cannot satisfy us at this point. It has many different meanings so it cannot be decided that way."[3]

The key to what Jesus means comes to us from the Gospel of John. Jesus says, "Do not *judge* according to appearance, but *judge* with righteous judgment" (Jn 7:24, emphasis added). Meaning, we are not to pronounce damnatory sentences on people, that's God's prerogative for people who reject Christ. Instead, we are to make a right assessment of a person's heart, and if need be call them to repentance (Mt 18:15-20). "Do not judge according to appearance, but judge with righteous judgment" (Jn 7:24).

D.A. Carson cogently explains this Scripture,

> In an age when Matthew 7:1('Do not judge or you too will be judged') has displaced John 3:16 as the only verse in the Bible the man in the street is likely to know, it is probably worth adding that Matthew 7:1 forbids judgmentalism, not moral discernment. By contrast, John 7:24 demands moral and theological discernment in the context of obedient faith (7:17),

[3] Lloyd-Jones, Studies in the Sermon on the Mount, 427.

> while excoriating self-righteous legalism and offering no sanction for censorious heresy-hunting.[4]

The point is, Christian's aren't to be judgmental Pharisees but they are to make judgment calls. They are to be humble Christ-loving fruit inspectors not prideful self-righteous mote-hunters.

This is what the risen Christ commanded the church at Thyatira to do because of sexual immorality and false prophecy that they were allowing to go on unchecked (Rev 2:20-25). Christ warned the church at Thyatira, and all of His churches, that if they didn't do something about it He would. To love someone enough to admonish them for sinning isn't easy, it's a labor of love. We cannot let sin go unchecked in the church. A failure to do so brings the guilt of sin on the whole church. Ultimately, how church discipline will play out is out of your hands. The question is: Can the one being disciplined endure God's correction by means of fellow believers?

This duty to protect the sheep includes exercising discipline for the preservation both of truth and duty. As the congregation is submissive and obedient, the pastor will be able to lead with joy and not grief, which is ultimately unprofitable for everyone. On occasion, the pastor and elders may have to discipline erring brethren who are living in unrepentant sin.

[4] Carson, The Gospel According to John, 317. This is by far one of the best commentaries on John's Gospel.

Part Four: Seven Core Directives

A pastor is God's man. Through the plurality of godly men, the Holy Spirit directs the people of God to accomplish His goals in the earth. Part of a pastor's ministry is therefore to direct the affairs of Christ's church. Here in part three, the aim will be to outline what constitutes the seven core activities a pastor directs in the life of the congregation: Corporate worship, preaching the Word, baptism and the Lord's Supper, dedications, ordinations, weddings, and funerals.

Chapter Seventeen: Corporate Worship

"Oh come, let us worship and bow down; let us kneel before the Lord our Maker. 7 For He is our God, and we are the people of His pasture, and the sheep of His hand." – Psalm 95:6-7

We were created in order to worship God. Worship is therefore central to the life of every saint, and vital to the existence of the Church. Worship according to the Bible is not just any kind we would like but that which is done, "In spirit and in truth" (John 4:23-24). In other words, worship that glorifies God is animated by his Spirit and informed by the truth of his revelation in Jesus Christ. In worship, "the saints do not merely seek God, they also find Him."[1] Worship is also a means of grace, whereby the saints receive spiritual nourishment, and are sent away rich.

As Thomas Watson once observed, praising God is one of the highest and purest acts of religion. "In praise, we act like angels." And the acceptable way of worshiping God has been instituted by God himself, that is, according to His revealed will. For example, the first and second commandments demonstrates God's particular care with regard to worship (Ex 20:2–6). The incident of the golden calf, as well as that of the deaths of Nadab and Abihu who offered "strange fire" (Lev 10), teach us that worship cannot be offered merely in accord with our own values and tastes.

Likewise, in the Book of Exodus, the tabernacle, which was at that time the central place of worship, was to be built and everything in it was to be done after the

---

[1] J.I. Packer, *A Quest for Godliness* (Wheaton: Crossway, 1990), 252.

pattern shown to Moses and the people (Ex 25:40). As all this indicates, God is to be worshipped according to His revealed will and not according to ways not prescribed in Scripture. Worship is of such importance that it must be carefully guarded by those whom God has called to lead His people. Pastors are to lead their congregations in worship in namely four ways.

In Justin's Apology, these four ways or elements of worship are brought out. Justin's First Apology is dated to between AD 155-157 and regarding worship observes:

> And on the day called **Sunday**, all who live in cities or in the country gather together to one place, and the memoirs of the apostles or the writings of the prophets are **read**, as long as time permits; then, when the reader has ceased, the president verbally **instructs**, and exhorts to the imitation of these good things. Then we all rise together and **pray**, and, as we before said, when our prayer is ended, **bread and wine and water are brought**, and the president in like manner offers prayers and thanksgivings, according to his ability, and the people assent, saying Amen (emphasis added).[1]

These elements mentioned by Justin consist of the basic framework of traditional worship. First, the Christians met on Sunday where they assembled to hear the Word read (read it). Second, the pastor instructs and exhorts them regarding the reading (preach it). Third, they rise to pray (pray it), and fourth, after the prayer bread first and then wine and water are brought (see it).

---

[1] Justin Martyr, *First Apology*, 67.

1. Worship through reading the Word. In 1 Timothy 4:13 Paul writes: "Till I come, give attention to reading, to exhortation, to doctrine." What Paul urged Timothy to do is every time he opened the Bible, he was to do so in the presence of the Author, as the very mouthpiece of the Author. The one who reads the Bible in public should therefore be one who is filled with the Spirit of God. Moreover, because the Bible is verbally inspired, the one reading it should ask for the help in speaking the text clearly with the aid of the Spirit. Ultimately, our goal should be to arrange for the people to have an encounter with the Word of God.

2. Worship through preaching and teaching the Word. Christ is our Mediator in worship. This is the true essence of worship. Christ as High Priesthood is the leader of our worship, and through him we approach the Father. This is what guarantees our acceptance. As we worship through preaching and teaching, Christ Himself feeds His sheep.

3. Worship through praying the Word. The Bible gives us examples of both public and private prayers. Prayer is an offering up of our needs to God. Prayer is therefore solemn and holy. Like other forms of worship in the church, the one praying should likewise be filled with and led by the Spirit of God.

Prayer proceeds from the Holy Spirit within the believer. The Holy Spirit literally prays within us, so that true prayer starts from the mediatorial throne of Christ, comes into the believer, and then goes back up to that throne with divine acceptance and power. In this vein, Doug Kelly observes,

> Although the main emphasis in our prayers must be on the clearly revealed will of God in Scripture, this

> does not mean that His secret will has no connection with our praying. On the contrary, when we pray on the basis of the revealed will, we are lining ourselves up with the person of God and thus with the secret purposes of God. His secret purposes are carried out through the praying of His saints on the basis of His revealed will in Scripture.[2]

Genuine worship flows from our hearts, and is therefore not an external activity. Our worship of God is not a meritorious work. Our worship is all about Christ and His once-for-all sacrifice of Himself for us so that we might become the righteousness of God (2 Cor 5:21).

4. <u>Worship through the visualizing the Word in the ordinances</u>. Our worship is not a human good work, but a gracious participation in the one Priesthood of Christ. Baptism and the Lord's Supper are therefore "visible gospels."

Worship is therefore mankind's highest calling, and as a pastor, guiding a congregation through worship is one of your greatest responsibilities and privileges. The pastor therefore must do all he can to ensure that God's people will "offer to God acceptable worship, with reverence and awe" (Heb. 12:28–29).

When Jesus tells us, we must worship the Father "in spirit and in truth," He is telling us at least two things: First, that the Father is a spiritual rather than a corporeal being, and that those who worship Him must do so in a spiritual rather than a material way. And two, a spiritual birth, regeneration is prerequisite for spiritual worship (Jn 3:5). Therefore, those who

---

[2] Doug Kelly, *If God Already Knows Why Pray*, 56-57.

worship Him must worship "in spirit" instead of a hypocritical worship (Mk 7:6-7).

In light of this, rather than saying, whatever is not commanded in Scripture, we are free to choose, rather we should disapprove of all modes of worship not expressly sanctioned by his Word. This view is known as the Regulative principle of worship. This principle states: "Whatever is commanded by God for worship is required, and whatever is not commanded by God is forbidden." Ligon Duncan summarizes this principle by saying, "the Regulative Principle teaches us to "read the Bible, preach the Bible, pray the Bible, sing the Bible, and see the Bible."[3]

Certainly, this raises some questions such as: Can we allow a blend of Christian worship music and hymns and/or psalms into our corporate worship without violating this rule? If the music is ministry, the answer should be yes. If the music is entertainment the answer most assuredly must be no. Commenting on this issue, John Frame acknowledges that some Christian worship music (CWM) is too simplistic and perhaps doesn't carry the weight of older hymns but believes that carefully-chosen CWM may be used along with traditional hymns.

In agreement with Frame, we do best to differentiate CWM with that of Christian contemporary music (CCM), which is often doctrinally vacant and more pop than worship. Such music, in the opinion of Frame, focuses more on the "talents of the leaders, their cleverness, skill, literary polish, pleasant personalities anything but the presence of the Lord himself."[4]

---

3 Duncan, Give Praise to God, 65.
4 John Frame, *Contemporary Worship Music*, 59.

Frame's argument against the use of CCM is well received especially in a day and age where Christians are divorcing themselves from historic Creeds and substituting of worship for "entertainment." Whereas the Word and Sacraments constituted the focal point of the ministry in the past, as Donald Bloesch notes, "the new emphasis is on personal sharing, visual aids, and contemporary music."[5]

As the New Testament teaches us, the place of true worship has now been universalized to any place where the Spirit resides in true worshipers (Jn 4:21-24), and Christ is the True Temple, and if we are in Him, then we are a part of it (1 Pet 2:4-5). The people of God are the new place of worship which replaced the Temple. As fellow workers with Christ, we are building God's temple. As Jesus ministers though us, we extend the holy sphere over all the earth. In this way, God's tabernacling presence expands spiritually through us as we minister to the world.

---

[5] Donald G. Bloesch, *The Church, Sacraments, Worship, Ministry, Mission* (Downers Grove: IVP, 2002), 35.

Chapter Eighteen: Sermons

"The motto of all true servants of God must be, 'We preach Christ; and him crucified.' A sermon without Christ in it is like a loaf of bread without any flour in it. No Christ in your sermon, sir? Then go home, and never preach again until you have something worth preaching." – Charles H. Spurgeon

A pastor is called to preach the Word (2 Tim 4:2). When live in a day and age when most ignore Paul's exhortation. "Instead of the Word of God," as John MacArthur rightly observes, "all too often from the pulpit come the uncertain sounds of political rhetoric, social commentary, and pop psychology. Such "persuasive words of [human] wisdom" (1 Cor 2:4) are a prostitution of the preacher's true calling."[1] However, a man committed to God's truth, handles God's Word rightly (2 Tim 2:15). This chapter deals specifically with the preparation and delivery of sermons.

When preparing a sermon, there are essentially three labors of the preacher: (1) the labor of understanding the Text; (2) the labor of knowing how to lay out the Text: and (3) the labor of communicating the Text. While doing this, consider the following:

1. The sermon must be derived from the Scripture. Always be textual.
2. The sermon must not deal with any text in isolation but should be derived from the whole counsel of God.
3. The sermon must include doctrinal content.

---

[1] John MacArthur, *Pastoral Ministry: How to Shepherd Biblically* (Nashville: Thomas Nelson, 2005), 18.

4. The sermon must be theological but not merely a lecture on theology, nor merely a class.
5. Preach the gospel – don't preach about the gospel.
6. Repetition in a sermon is good.
7. A sermon should always be expository.
8. A sermon should: (1) explain the context, (2) examine important words, and (3) draw out the lesson(s).
9. Apply the application as you go along.
10. Always end with a note of application or exhortation.
11. A sermon should be an entity, a complete whole.
12. The hope and expectation of every sermon is: (1) The conversion of sinners, and (2) the edification of saints.

The primary task of the church is to preach and teach mankind the only remedy, the only cure, and that is salvation by Christ alone, by grace alone, through faith alone for the glory of God alone. Man's real trouble is that he is a rebel against God and consequently under the wrath of God. He is dead to the life of God and in a continual state of darkness. This is the bad news that must be presented before the good news, i.e., mankind apart from Christ is dead, defiled, and damned. These are the terms that express the biblical diagnosis of man's essential trouble. Christians are people who have been called out of darkness into God's marvelous light.

In light on this, the primary task of the church is not to educate man or to even heal him physically or psychologically (all the while God still does this). In this vein, Spurgeon observes: "The Spirit of God bears no witness to Christless sermons. Leave Jesus out of your preaching, and the Holy Spirit will never come upon you. Why should he? Has he not come on purpose that he may testify of Christ? Did not Jesus say, 'He shall glorify me: for he shall receive of mine, and shall show it unto you'? Yes, the subject was Christ, and nothing but Christ, and such is the teaching which the Spirit of God will own. Be it ours never to wander from this central point: may we determine to know nothing among men but Christ and his cross."

Moreover, the primary task of the church is not to make man happy or make him good (These are things that accompany salvation). When the church accomplishes her task correctly, men are educated, become happy and morally good, and in God's time are physically and psychologically healed according to His will.

Preaching the Word is prophesying in the name and on behalf of Christ. Through preaching those who hear are called into the state of grace, and preserved in it. Preaching is therefore truth, mediated through personality. The preacher should therefore have a sense of authority and anointing and therefore be gripped by what he is saying. Avoid light without heat or heat without light. Preaching is theology coming through a man who is on fire. What is the chief end of preaching? It is to give men and women a sense of God and His presence.

Preaching is therefore the most amazing, and the most thrilling activity that one can ever be engaged in, because of all that is holds out for all of us in the present and because of the glorious endless possibilities in an eternal future. As Lloyd-Jones observes, "It is a great matter to understand what it is to be a preacher, and how preaching should be done. Affective sermons are the offspring of study, of discipline, of prayer, and especially of the unction of the Holy Ghost."

There are four axioms of preaching: First, is the primacy of the intellect. As J.I. Packer relates, "Everyman's first duty in relation to the Word of God is to understand it; and every preacher's first duty is to explain it." [1] Second, the belief in the supreme importance of preaching. "Nothing honors God more than the faithful declaration and obedient hearing of his truth." [2] Third, is the belief in the life-giving power of the Holy Scripture. "Better not preach at all than preach beyond the Bible." [3] And fourth, is the belief in the Sovereignty of the Holy Spirit. "Man's task is simply to be faithful in teaching the Word; it is God's work to convince of its truth and write it on the heart."[4]

And above all, when the Holy Spirit comes upon you in preaching, let go. "The 'demonstration of the Spirit' (1 Cor 2:4) becomes a reality when, in preaching, the minister of the Word conducts himself in such a way that everyone — even those who are ignorant of the gospel and are unbelievers — recognize that it is not so much the preacher who is speaking, but the Spirit of God in him and by him (Mic 3:8; 1 Cor 2:4; 14:24, 25; 4:19,20). This is what makes his ministry living and powerful (Luke 11:27)."

What makes preaching "preaching?" Make it memorable, compelling, and arresting. Make it structured. Make it natural and "faithful" to the passage.

---

[1] J.I Packer, A Quest for Godliness, 281.

[2] Ibid.

[3] Ibid, 282.

[4] Ibid,73.

Exegesis

A text without a context is a pretext for a proof text. What Carson means is we must understand the text and understand who it was written to and then take that text, find the meaning and application for our lives. The point is, without understanding the context, you won't know the trajectory of where the Word of God is taking that passage. Preaching the truth means committing ourselves to a lifetime of exegesis. What is exegesis? Exegesis is the discovery of the intended meaning of a passage of Scripture. It's the author's intended meaning, but also the "Author's" intended meaning. It's the meaning intended for the original hearers, but also the one intended for us. The English exegesis comes to us from the Greek word ἐξήγησις *exegesis* which means to lead out or draw out.

Why is exegesis so important? Without thorough exegesis we will preach what we think the Word is saying rather than what it is actually saying. Without exegesis, we do what called eisegesis. Eisegesis is when a reader imposes their interpretation of the text. Without exegesis, we will be preaching our own ideas rather than the Word itself.

For the task of exegesis, there are essentially three easy-to-remember rules to guide us: (1) Examine the whole book first, (2) study the passage itself, and (3) refer to the rest of the Scriptures.

First, examine the whole book first. Step into the writer's shoes and ask: What sort of world is he living in? Who is writing" To whom is he writing? What is his purpose? As we consider this, we should also consider the type of literature he is writing. Whether it be history, prophecy, poetry, apocalyptic, wisdom literature, epistles (letters), etc.

Second, from there we move to study the passage itself. We may ask: Where does the passage fall in the book? Does it contain any figurative language? Does the passage contain simile (Ps 103:13, Prov 26:14, Is 53:7, Matt 23:37)? Does it contain metaphor (Ps 23:1-2, Mal 3:10, Eph 2:19-20)? Parables (Mt 13:31-32, 33, 44, 45-46)? Allegory (2 Sam 12:1-6, Ezek 23, Mt 13:24-30, 36-43)? As we consider these points, we might ask: What is the mood of the passage? What about the tense used in the verbs?

Thirdly, we should refer to the rest of Scripture. As we do that, the following suggestions will help:

1. Use the clear to interpret the obscure (Rev 20:1-6).
2. Use the whole to interpret the part (1 Cor 7).
3. Use the New Testament to interpret the Old Testament (Amos 9:11-15/Acts 15:13-16/Joel 2:28-32/ Acts 2:16- 21).
4. Remember Christ is the central focus of the whole Bible (Lk 24:27,44 Jn 16:13-14).
5. Remember that the whole Bible is a revelation (2 Tim 3:15-17).
6. Remember that the Bible is the self-revelation of the covenant God to His people (Lk 24:44)
7. Expect to encounter paradoxes (Matt 11:25-30).
8. Remember that not everything is revealed (Dt 29:29; Pro 25:2).
9. Remember that your own understanding is limited (1 Cor 3:1-3; Heb 5:9-14).
10. Above all, ask the Author for understanding (Psalm 119:18; James 1:5).

Above all, said Charles Spurgeon, you are not really preaching the gospel if you leave Christ out. "If He be omitted, it is not the gospel. You may invite men to listen to your message, but you are only inviting them to gaze upon an empty table unless Christ is the very center and substance of all that you set before them."

Expository Preaching

The Directory for the Publick Worship of God, written in 1645 by the Westminster Assembly, raised a central point when it admonished preachers to ensure that when they preached the sermon should be "a truth contained in or grounded on the text, so that the hearers may discern how God teaches from it." In other words, preaching must enable those who hear it to understand their Bibles.

This is the essence of what the Apostle Paul urged Timothy to do when he said: "preach the word" (2 Tim 4:2). Thus, the preacher is to make God's Word known and make it understandable. As he does so, he is to limit himself to Scripture, without adding or subtracting from it. This type of preaching is known as "expository," which is the opening up and explaining of a passage of Scripture. Paul charged Timothy to present himself to God "as one approved, a worker who has no need to be ashamed, rightly handling the word of truth" (2 Tim. 2:15). The word that is translated "to handle" or "to divide" actually means "to cut" *orthotomeo*. Timothy was to make a straight cut through the Word of God and not deviate to the left or to the right. He was to "preach the word" by expounding the particular passage he was preaching on.

J.I. Packer writes, "To recover the old, authentic, biblical gospel, and to bring our preaching and practice back into line with it, is perhaps our most pressing present need."[5] "The preacher's task, in other words, is to display Christ; to explain man's need of Him, His sufficiency to save, and His offer of Himself in the promises as Savior to all who truly turn to Him."[6]

As pastors, we are responsible for God's people being fed. As Spurgeon put it, "I do believe we slander Christ when we think we are to draw the people by something else but the preaching of Christ crucified. We must be prepared and then preach with conviction and passion whether it be to ten or to a thousand.

---

[5] Owen, The Death of Death in the Death of Christ, 2.
[6] Ibid, 16.

Chapter Nineteen: Baptism and the Lord's Supper

"O Sovereign Lord, holy and true, how long before you will judge and avenge our blood on those who dwell on the earth" (Rev 6:10)?

The Lord Jesus gives His Church lasting signs. These are baptism and the Lord's Supper. These visible signs, that are also means of grace, relate the corresponding truth that they signify. Just as the Lord's Supper correlates to the Messianic banquet at the end of time, baptism shows, by sign, the manner in which believers are buried with Christ in His death and raised in His resurrection power to walk a new life, free from the guilt of sin and the condemning power of death.

As has been said, the church is the visible witness of God. This is how the world sees Jesus – in the church. Yet, however visible the people of God may be to the world at any particular time, it remains invisible, known only to God. Peter Craigie reminds us that, "whereas the old covenant had an external form in the nation state, the new covenant would be marked by an inner work of God in man's heart."[146] This inner work on man's heart, "the answer of a good conscience toward God" (1 Pet 3:21), is made visible in both baptism and in the Lord's Supper.

These sacraments or ordinances are signs, symbols, and testaments. Signs point, symbols resemble, and testaments testify. Baptism is a sign showing that the true believer has been once-for-all incorporated into

[146] Craigie, The Problem of War in the Old Testament, 79.

Christ.[147] That his sins have been forgiven. It shows our union with Christ in His death and our rising together with Him, by regeneration through His resurrection, to walk in newness of life (Rom 6:4; 1 Pet 1:3).

Baptism is a symbol resembling our death to the world and sin's dominion. It corresponds and relates in graphic form to Christ's sufferings and death for our redemption and righteousness. It is the visible gospel. Further, baptism is a testament, in that it bears witness or testifies to the believer's good conscience toward God (1 Pet 3:21) – removal of the guilt of sin through repentance and faith; love for Christ and his subjection to Him (lordship). John Calvin writes, "Baptism is a kind of entrance into the Church, an initiation into the faith, and the Lord's Supper the constant ailment by which Christ spiritually feeds his family of believers."[148] Thus, baptism reflects our once-for-all union with Christ, the Lord's Supper reflects our continuous participation in Him. Christ instituted the Eucharist or Communion so to help Christians grasp the reality of their union with Him in some measure.

The word "communion" κοινωνία koinonia means participation and fellowship. God's people are one body in Christ. Christ indwells His church in the fellowship of the Spirit.[149] Thus, Christians have fellowship with Christ and each other through the Holy Spirit. Perfected fellowship with God is the goal of human history.[150] The world should see this fellowship

---

[147] Biblical signs are physical and temporal phenomenon that have corresponding spiritual and eternal significance. Signs σημεῖον semeon produce faith in those who have ears to hear the gospel (Mt 13:10-17).

[148] Calvin, Institutes of the Christian Religion, Book IV, 19.

[149] Clowney, The Church, 29.

[150] Ibid, 173.

in the church. The Lord's Supper is a sign, symbol, and testament to this truth.

After repentance towards God and faith towards the Lord Jesus Christ, the believer is to publicly proclaim his identity with Christ by water baptism, in the Name of the Father, Son, and Holy Spirit. It is an act of obedience symbolizing the believer's faith in a crucified, buried, and risen Saviour, the believer's death to sin, the burial of the old life, and the resurrection to walk in newness of life in Christ Jesus. It is a testimony to his faith in the final resurrection of the dead. Being a church ordinance, it is prerequisite to the privileges of church membership and to the Lord's Supper.

The Lord's Supper is a symbolic act of obedience whereby members of the church, through partaking of the bread and the fruit of the vine, memorialize the death of the Christ and anticipate His second coming. Communion is to be taken frequently and offered to all believers except those who are living in unrepentant rebellion or immorality. The communion elements are symbols of Christ's body and blood and are useful to the exercise of faith in the Person of Jesus Christ as the only means of absolving guilt, shame, and punishment of sin.

Christian baptism is a sign from God that signifies inward cleansing and remission of sins (Acts 22:16; 1 Cor 6:11; Eph 5:25–27), Spirit-wrought regeneration and new life (Titus 3:5), and the abiding presence of the Holy Spirit as God's seal testifying and guaranteeing that one will be kept safe in Christ forever (1 Cor 12:13; Eph 1:13–14). Baptism carries these meanings because first and fundamentally it signifies union with Christ in his death, burial, and resurrection (Rom 6:3–7; Col

2:11–12); and this union with Christ is the source of every element in our salvation (1 John 5:11–12). Receiving the sign in faith assures the persons baptized that God's gift of new life in Christ is freely given to them.[151]

Baptism Order of Service:

The pastor and other church leaders should take time with each candidate to assure themselves that the person desiring baptism is genuinely saved.

(Pastor): *"Have you _____ (name of person being baptized) repented of your sins and believe in Jesus Christ as your Lord and Savior?"*

(Person being baptized): *"I do."*

(Pastor): "_________ (Full name of the person being baptized), *upon your confession of faith in the Lord Jesus Christ as your personal Savior, I baptize you in the name of the Father, and of the Son, and of the Holy Spirit."*

The pastor then briefly immerses the person and then helps them exit the water.

At the close of the service, or soon afterward, the pastor should present the person with a certificate of baptism.

---

[151] J. I. Packer,

Lord's Supper Order of Service:

The pastor should ensure that the preparation of the table and the elements are in the hands of responsible persons. The pastor should also ensure that the linen and utensils being used are clean. Additionally, the place given to the Lord's Supper should never be merely an appendage to the service, rather it should be the theme.

The pastor invites the people to partake of the elements and says something to this effect:

(Pastor): "*At our church, we practice an open form of communion, which means you are freely invited to partake of the Lord's Supper provided that you are indeed a believer in the Lord Jesus Christ and have received Him as Savior and Lord. And we will take the elements together.*"

(The pastor then takes the bread and hands it to the ushers/deacons to deliver to the people. Then the pastor takes the fruit of the vine and gives it to the ushers/deacons to be delivered to the people).

During the distribution of the elements, an instrumentalist may play softly, while the congregation meditates quietly.

Once everyone who is taking the Supper has the elements, the pastor takes the bread, hold it up and says:

(Pastor): *"The Lord Jesus, the same night he was betrayed, took bread; and when He had given thanks, He broke it and said "Take, eat, this is My body which is given for you: Do this in remembrance of Me" (Lk 22:19).*

The pastor invites participants to take the bread.

Then in the same manner, the pastor holds up the cup and says:

(Pastor): '*"Then He took the cup, and gave thanks, and gave it to them, saying, "Drink from it, all of you. For this is My blood of the new covenant, which is shed for many for the remission of sins"' (Mt 26:27-28).*

The pastor then invites participants to take the juice.

After a brief silence, the pastor should conclude the Supper with a prayer.

(If holders are not provided in the pews for empty cups, the servers should return with the empty trays to collect them or if they are disposable cups, a container to collect them should be provided).

Chapter Twenty: Dedication

"Now when the days of her purification according to the law of Moses were completed, they brought Him to Jerusalem to present Him to the Lord" (Lk 2:22).

The blessing and dedicating of an infant is a public declaration of the parent(s) before God and man that means at least four things: First, it shows that the parent(s) acknowledge the child as a great gift of the Lord (Ps 127:3). Second, it shows that the parent(s) acknowledge the responsibility to raise the child in the training and admonition of the Lord (Eph 6:4). Third, it shows that the parent(s) have made a commitment to shepherd the heart of the child as the baby grows into adulthood. And fourth, it means that the congregation commits to assist the parent(s) in this effort.

Order of Service:

During the ceremony, the pastor should ask the parent(s) to bring the child to the front of the church.

(Pastor): *"Do you* ______ (parent) *vow before God and the congregation that you will raise* _____ (child's name) *in the Christian faith, that you will be his or her example, and that you will train your child in Christian disciplines of prayer, Bible reading and church attendance."*

(The pastor then holds and blesses the child).

(Pastor): *"Now may the Lord bless you and keep you; the Lord make His face shine upon you, and be gracious to you; The Lord lift up His countenance upon you, and give you peace. And in this way, they shall place My name on the children of Israel, and I will bless them" (Num 6:23-27).*

The pastor then hands the child back to the parent(s) and gives them dedication certificate. When the parent(s) and child are seated, the pastor makes a concluding prayer.

Chapter Twenty-One: Ordination and Installation

"O Sovereign Lord, holy and true, how long before you will judge and avenge our blood on those who dwell on the earth" (Rev 6:10)?

Ordaining a man to the gospel ministry is both a high and holy distinction. As Gods' man, it means you have been called to a life of service to Christ and His sheep. Ordination is the authoritative admission of one duly called to an office in the Church of God, accompanied with prayer and the laying on of hands, to which it is proper to add the giving of the right hand of fellowship. According to the Scriptures, it is a special charge. Moreover, no man should be ordained unless it be to the performance of a definite work.

The ordination process of the church is an earthly expression of God's eternal ordination upon the life of the one being set apart for ministry. After a man is thoroughly examined as to his competency in the Holy Scriptures, his life and faith, is to be ordained as a minister of the gospel. The following outlines are intended to assist in the performance of ordination and installation services:

Ordination:

The applicant to the ministry is to be examined by the Presbytery (council of elders) on matters pertaining to his faith and doctrine, as well as his motives for seeking the ministry. If the examination proves to be satisfactory, the Presbytery shall receive him under its care after the following manner:

Moderator:

1. *"Do you promise in reliance upon the grace of God to maintain a becoming Christian character, and to be diligent and faithful in making full preparation for the sacred ministry?"*

2. *"Do you promise to submit yourself to the proper supervision of the Presbytery in matters that concern your preparation for the ministry?"*

If these questions be answered in the affirmative, the moderator, or someone appointed by him, shall give the candidate a brief charge; and the proceeding shall close with prayer.

Installation of a Pastor:

Moderator:

1. *"Do you believe the Scriptures of the Old and New Testaments to be the inerrant Word of God, the only infallible rule of faith and practice?"*

2. *"Do you sincerely receive and adopt the Statement of Faith of ____ Church, as containing the system of doctrine taught in the Holy Scriptures; and do you further promise that if at any time you find yourself out of accord with any of the fundamentals of this system of doctrine, you will on your own initiative, make known the change which has taken place in your views since the assumption of this ordination vow?"*

3. "Do you approve of the form of government and discipline of _____ Church, in conformity with the general principles of Biblical polity?"

4. "Do you promise to be zealous and faithful in maintaining the truths of the Gospel and the purity and peace and unity of the Church, whatever persecution or opposition may arise unto you on that account?"

5. "Do you promise to be faithful and diligent in the exercise of all your duties as a Christian and a minister of the Gospel, whether personal or relational, private or public?"

6. "Do you promise to endeavor by the grace of God to adorn the profession of the Gospel in your manner of life, and to walk with exemplary piety before the flock of which God shall make you overseer?"

7. "Are you now willing to take the charge of this church, agreeable to your declaration when accepting their call? And do you, relying upon God for strength, promise to discharge to it the duties of pastor?"

Installation of an Elder or Deacon:

1. "Do you believe the Scriptures of the Old and New Testaments to be the inerrant Word of God, the only infallible rule of faith and practice?"

2. "Do you sincerely receive and adopt the statement of faith of ____ Church, as containing the system of doctrine taught in the Holy Scriptures; and do you further promise that if at any time you find yourself out of accord with any of the fundamentals of this system of doctrine, you will, on your own initiative, make known the change which has taken place in your views since the assumption of this ordination vow?"

3. "Do you approve of the form of government and discipline of _____Church, in conformity with the general principles of biblical polity?"

4. "Do you accept the office of ruling elder (or deacon, as the case may be) in this church, and promise faithfully to perform all the duties thereof, and to endeavor by the grace of God to adorn the profession of the Gospel in your life, and to set a worthy example before the Church of which God has made you an officer?"

5. "Do you promise to strive for the purity, peace, unity and edification of the Church?"

Chapter Twenty-Two: Weddings

"For this reason a man shall leave his father and mother and be joined to his wife, and the two shall become one flesh" (Eph 5:21).

A biblical marriage is one in which the husband and wife are committed to God and committed to each other. Marriage is the lifetime covenant commitment in which one man and one woman unite together under God. It is the God-ordained institution on which the family, as well as society as a whole is founded. God created marriage for the mutual help of husband and wife, to provide mankind with a legitimate issue, to give the Church a holy progeny. Marriage also reveals the relationship between Christ and His church. A man's greatest treasure is his wife, she is a gift from the Lord (Pro 18:22). A biblical marriage is one in which the husband and wife are committed to God and committed to each other.

Premarital Counseling

Being invited to officiate a wedding ceremony is a great honor for a pastor. In preparation, the pastor should arrange some premarital counseling for the couple, and acquaint himself with the local and State laws. There are at least three main reasons for premarital counseling: (1) It opens a dialogue about the couple's marriage; (2) it assesses areas for growth in the relationship; and (3) enables a couple to accurately assess their compatibility for marriage.

Studies show the chances of divorce for newly married couples are between somewhere between 40-50%. In fact, couples entering their second marriage raises this chance to 60%. However, premarital counseling has shown to reduce the chances of divorce by 30%. The Bible's view of marriage is *dependent*, *interdependent*, and *intimate*. When conducting premarital counseling the following as a minimum should be discussed:

1. *Dependence*: Dependence in marriage means both the husband and wife understand they are both completely dependent on the Lord for everything, especially salvation. A biblical marriage is one in which the husband and wife are committed to God and committed to each other.

2. *Interdependence*: As image bearers of God, men and women have equal dignity and value in God's eyes. Men and women were created with different gender roles. A husband and wife are called to leave their family of origin and to cleave to their new spouse (Eph 5:21). The two become "one flesh." The relationship between Christ and the church models for husbands and wives how they are to relate to one another.

None of us are perfect. As a product of the environment we grew up in, we carry our experiences with us. These experiences shape our world view and can influence all our relationships (with God and others). The goal is to be honest about negative experiences in our past so as to better understand each other and as we work toward spiritual wellness in those areas (1 Peter 5:7).

The marriage relationship should be compatible in respect not only to world view but to personality type. The goal is to know each other's personality and temperament so as to better communicate and understand one another. Effective communication is one of the keys to a lasting marriage (1 Pet 3:1-3). Something that could be discussed here is active listening and assertiveness. Additionally, finances should be discussed. What are their views on a budget? Tithing? Saving for the future? Also, what are the couple's aspirations for the future and especially children?

3. *Intimacy* – Finally, discuss intimacy. God gifted most men and women to desire sexual intimacy and children (1 Cor 7:9). Physical attraction and intimacy are therefore gifts from God and a blessing to be enjoyed in marriage. A healthy biblical intimacy involves physical, emotional, and spiritual aspects. Important here is to discuss managing sexual temptation and avoiding sex before being married (1 Cor 6:18).

According to the Bible, marriage is not merely a "committed interdependent partnership between consenting adults," marriage is one in which the husband and wife are committed to God and committed to each other. The goal is to have a marriage that glorifies God (1 Cor 10:31).

Wedding Ceremony

When officiating a wedding, a pastor's poise is the key to the whole ceremony's equilibrium. As the pastor is calm, so too will he impart calmness and inspire confidence in others. The following is a suggested order of service:

The Announcement

(Pastor): *"'In the beginning God created the heavens and the earth. God saw all that He had made and it was very good. And the Lord God, seeing that is was better for the man to not be alone said, "I will make a helper suitable for him."'*

"Then the Lord God made a woman from the rib He had taken out of the man, and He brought her to the man. And the man said, "This is now bone of my bones and flesh of my flesh."

"In that act, God Himself preformed the first wedding ceremony, providing us with the example to follow."

"Dearly beloved, we are gathered here today in the sight of God, several thousand years after the first wedding, to join this man and this woman in holy matrimony."

"Who gives this woman to be married to this man?"

(Father of the Bride): *"Her mother and I do."*

Wedding Sermon (About five minutes):

Declaration of Intent:

"(Groom) _____ *and* (Bride) ______, *now that you have heard God's message concerning marriage, do you agree with it and do you commit yourselves to each other in accordance with it?"*

Each answers: *"I do."*

Exchange of Vows:

(Pastor): *"In the presence of God and before these witnesses I now invite you to exchange your vows."*

(Groom): *"I take you, _____ (Bride), to be my wife and I promise before God and all who are present here to be your loving and faithful husband, as long as our lives shall last. I will love you and give myself up for you, as Christ loved the church and gave Himself up for her. I will serve you with tenderness and respect, and encourage you to develop the gifts that God has given you."*

(Bride): *"I take you, _____ (Groom), to be my husband and I promise before God and all who are present here to be your loving and faithful wife, as long as our lives shall last. I will love you and submit to you, as the church loves and submits to Christ. I will serve you with tenderness and respect, and encourage you to develop the gifts that God has given you."*

Exchange of Rings

(Pastor): *"The ring is a continuous circle that symbolizes the unending nature of the love and commitment that bind one man and one woman together in marriage. The act of giving rings, therefore, serves as a visible reminder of the marriage vows. Moreover, the wedding ring is worn throughout marriage as a symbol that informs others that this person has committed themselves to a lifelong covenant to another."*

(Groom): "_____ *(Bride), I give you this ring as a symbol of our covenant in Christ."*

(Bride): "_____ *(Groom), I give you this ring as a symbol of our covenant in Christ."*

Pronouncement

(Pastor): *"Now by the authority vested in me by God, I now pronounce you, husband and wife, in the name of the Father, and of the Son, and of the Holy Spirit. Amen."*

"You may kiss the bride."

Presentation

"Ladies and gentlemen, it is my pleasure to present to you, Mr. and Mrs. ________."

Prayer

"Most gracious and holy God, we pray that You will bless this union of _____ (Groom) and ______ (Bride). Uphold them by Your mighty arm. Keep them faithful to you and each other. Bless them with long life, children, and much joy. In Jesus' name I pray. Amen."

Benediction

"Now, may the Lord bless you and keep you. The Lord make His face shine upon you, and be gracious to you. The Lord lift up His countenance upon you, and give you peace."

Recessional

Bride and Groom
Bridesmaids and Groomsmen
Bride's Parents
Groom's Parents
Bride's Grandparents

Dismissal

Officiant makes announcements and dismisses the guests.

Chapter Twenty-Three: Funerals

"O Sovereign Lord, holy and true, how long before you will judge and avenge our blood on those who dwell on the earth" (Rev 6:10)?

The most difficult time in ministry is ministering to a person whose loved one has just passed away. In fact, no demand on a pastor is greater than the call to minster to bereaved members of his congregation and to officiate the funeral service. When notified, a pastor should console a grieving member of the congregation as soon as possible. And at a reasonable moment, he should ascertain the wishes of the family concerning the funeral arrangements. Additionally, the congregation should be informed of the death as soon as possible to assist in comforting the grieving family.

When conducting the funeral, the attitude of the pastor is of the utmost importance. John Bisagno observes, "Nothing has helped me more than this: Imagine the person in the casket is your mom or dad. The deceased may be a virtual stranger to you but to their family, he or she is life's dearest treasure."[1] As to the point if the deceased was a believer or not, Bisagno opines "if the person was a believer, rejoice. If not, ignore it and comfort the family. If you are not certain, be vague about the spiritual condition of the deceased but clear about the gospel."[2]

---

[1] John Bisagno *Pastor's Handbook* (Nashville, TN: B & H, 2011), 124.
[2] Ibid.

Funeral Ceremony

The funeral service should have order and dignity. A pianist or other instrumentalist should begin playing softly about fifteen minutes before the service is scheduled to begin.

The Announcement

(Pastor): *"We are gathered here today in memory of our beloved friend, _______. We are gathered here to honor his/her life, to cherish his/her memory, and we share his/her hope that he/she has now realized, namely to be absent from the body and present with the Lord."*

"From the Scriptures we draw great comfort:

(Scripture 1): *Job Chapter 19:25-27 tells us: "For I know that my Redeemer lives, and He shall stand at last on the earth; and after my skin is destroyed, this I know, that in my flesh I shall see God, whom I shall see for myself, and my eyes shall behold, and not another."*

(Scripture 2): *Likewise, the Apostle Paul, in steadfast comfort and hope declared in 2 Timothy 4:7-8: "I have fought the good fight, I have finished the race, I have kept the faith. Finally, there is laid up for me the crown of righteousness, which the Lord, the righteous Judge, will give to me on that Day, and not to me only but also to all who have loved His appearing."*

Invocation

"God our Father, you are our refuge and strength, our very present help in trouble, You have been our dwelling place throughout all generations, we praise Thee O God our Father, for you have loved us and sent your Son Jesus Christ to redeem us, to wash our sins away in His own blood. Lord still our hearts and minds, give us grace for this present hour to comfort us now in our time of need with the love of Christ. We ask this in Jesus' name. Amen."

Hymn (*Because He Lives*):

Sermon (about ten minutes):

Committal Prayer

"God our Father, you are our refuge and strength, our very present help in trouble, You have been our dwelling place throughout all generations. We praise You, for you have loved us and sent your Son Jesus Christ to redeem us, to wash our sins away in His own blood. O Mighty God, we commend the soul of our brother/sister, and we commit his/her body to the ground, earth to earth, ashes to ashes, dust to dust; in the sure and certain hope of the Resurrection unto eternal life, through our Lord Jesus Christ, at whose coming in glorious majesty to judge the world, the earth and the sea shall give up their dead; and the corruptible bodies of those who rest in him shall be changed, and made like unto his own glorious body; according to the mighty working whereby he is able to subdue all things unto himself. "

"We thank you that you have taken _____ to be with you in glory, and now O Lord we pray for ourselves and ask that You still our hearts and minds, help us, Father, to walk by faith and not by sight, with our trust in Him who said, "Do not be afraid. I am the Alpha and Omega, the beginning and the end, the First and the Last. I am the living One; I was dead, and behold I am alive forever and ever! And I hold the keys of death and Hell."

"Lord, give us grace for this present hour. Comfort us now in our time of need with the love of Christ. Help us to view all things in light of eternity, waiting for the coming of our Lord Jesus Christ, listening for the trumpet call, hastening unto the new heavens and earth."

Hymn (*When We All Get to Heaven*):

Family Recessional and Exit

At the Graveside

(Pastor): *"Friends, we are gathered at the final resting place of all that is mortal of _______ (Full name). Brother/sister, we now commit your body to the ground in the sure and certain hope that it will rise again on that glory day when Jesus Christ returns. Therefore, rest in peace upon the bosom of the Lord."*

Part Five: Pastoral Resources

Pastors are called to feed Christ's sheep with the Word of God. The goal of this section is to provide you with various pastoral resources that will anchor you to the Church's roots and aid you in the preparation and delivery of sermons.

Chapter Twenty-Four: Creeds and Confessions

"The Bible is the Word of God to man; the Creed is man's answer to God." – Philip Schaff

The word "creed" comes to us from the Latin word "credo" which means I believe. Creeds are summaries of the great doctrines of the Bible. It is for this reason that they are most useful as they keep us on track and out of error. This chapter contains two creeds and one statement of faith which the Church has believed and taught for the past sixteen centuries.

The Apostle's Creed

I believe in God, the Father Almighty, the Creator of heaven and earth, and in Jesus Christ, His only Son, our Lord: Who was conceived of the Holy Spirit, born of the Virgin Mary, suffered under Pontius Pilate, was crucified, died, and was buried.

He descended into hell. [1] The third day He arose again from the dead. He ascended into heaven and sits at the right hand of God the Father Almighty, whence He shall come to judge the living and the dead. I believe in the Holy Spirit, the holy catholic [2] church, the communion of saints, the forgiveness of sins, the resurrection of the body, and life everlasting. Amen

End Notes:

1. "Descended into hell" does not refer to literally going down into the bowels of hell itself to be subject to the devil. Rather, it is a poetic way of stating that Christ truly and assuredly died on the cross, and His body remained under the power of death for three days.

2. The word "catholic" refers not to the Roman Catholic Church, but to the universal church of the Lord Jesus Christ. Catholic *katholikos* means universal in Greek.

The Apostles' Creed was not written by the Biblical Disciples. The name is deemed this as a sum and substance of the early Apostolic teaching which the disciples would have held to. Earliest version found is A.D. 215. The current version is circa 542 A.D.

The Nicene Creed
381 A.D.

I believe in one God, the Father Almighty, maker of heaven and earth, and of all things visible and invisible; And in one Lord Jesus Christ, the only begotten Son of God, begotten of his Father before all worlds, God of God, Light of Light, very God of very God, begotten, not made, being of one substance with the Father; by whom all things were made; who for us men and for our salvation came down from heaven, and was incarnate by the Holy Ghost of the Virgin Mary, and was made man; and was crucified also for us under Pontius Pilate; he suffered and was buried; and the third day he rose again according to the Scriptures, and ascended into heaven, and sitteth on the right hand of the Father; and he shall come again, with glory, to judge both the quick and the dead; whose kingdom shall have no end.

And I believe in the Holy Ghost, the Lord, and Giver of Life, who proceedeth from the Father and the Son; who with the Father and the Son together is worshipped and glorified; who spake by the Prophets. And I believe one holy Catholic and Apostolic Church; I acknowledge one baptism for the remission of sins; and I look for the resurrection of the dead, and the life of the world to come. Amen.

End Notes:

1. The Nicene Creed is formed on the basis of the Apostles' Creed. The clauses relating to the consubstantial divinity of Christ were contributed by the great Council held in Nicaea in A.D. 325; those relating to the divinity and personality of the Holy Ghost added by the Second Ecumenical Council, held at Constantinople in A.D.381.

2. The filioque clause, "and the Son," was added by the Council of the Western Church held at Toledo, Spain in A.D. 569. In its present form it is the Creed of the whole Christian Church, the Greek Church (Orthodox) rejecting only the last added clause (Hodge, *A Short History of Creeds and Confessions*, 4).

The Definition of Chalcedon

Oct 22, 451 AD

We, then, following the holy Fathers, all with one consent, teach men to confess one and the same Son, our Lord Jesus Christ, the same perfect in Godhead and also perfect in manhood; truly God and truly man, of a reasonable [rational] soul and body; consubstantial [coessential] with the Father according to the Godhead, and consubstantial with us according to the Manhood; in all things like unto us, without sin; begotten before all ages of the Father according to the Godhead, and in these latter days, for us and for our salvation, born of the Virgin Mary, the Mother of God, according to the Manhood; one and the same Christ, Son, Lord, ***Only-begotten****, to be acknowledged in two natures,* ***inconfusedly, unchangeably, indivisibly, inseparably****; the distinction of natures being by no means taken away by the union, but rather the property of each nature being preserved, and concurring in one Person and one Subsistence, not parted or divided into two persons, but one and the same Son, and only begotten, God the Word, the Lord Jesus Christ, as the prophets from the beginning [have declared] concerning him, and the Lord Jesus Christ himself has taught us, and the Creed of the holy Fathers has handed down to us.*

End Notes:

The Chalcedonian Definition, repudiated the notion of a single nature in Christ, and declared that He has two natures in one person and hypostasis; it also insists on the completeness of his two natures: Godhead and manhood.

Chapter Twenty-Five: Principles of Biblical Interpretation

"Where Scripture has not spoken, we are wisest to be silent."
– Bernard Ramm

Pastors are called to feed Christ's sheep with the Word of God. By preaching and teaching God's Word, a pastor delivers a message from God to God's people. As he communicates the truths of God's Word, the pastor should always aim at clearly interpreting the passage at hand so that the thoughts that stir the minds and hearts of the people are God's thoughts.

The Apostle Paul urged Timothy and all preachers of the Word to, "Do your best to present yourself to God as one approved, a worker who has no need to be ashamed, rightly handling the word of truth" (2 Tim 2:15). This Scripture's primary purpose is to remind those who preach the Word to rightly handle the Scriptures. Pastors are called to make a straight-cutting of the Scripture, a handling aright. The man who uses God's Word doesn't mutilate it, or pervert it, or even water it down, but he interprets Scripture aright in the light of Scripture.

The fundamental that should govern all biblical interpretation is called the analogy of faith, which basically means that Scripture is its own interpreter. In other words, interpreting the Scripture is to be done according to Scripture. What this means is, the way we interpret the meaning of a particular verse in the Bible is by the overall teaching of the Bible. So, when one passage is unclear to us, we should understand it by way of another similar passage that bring clarity.

Secondly, because we are in possession of the verbally inspired Word of God, the Bible is therefore to be interpreted according to the ordinary rules of language. This means the Bible should be read literally, until the Bible itself uses symbols that lead us do understand a passage in a symbolic or allegorical way.

The following six principles, which follow the acronym **LIGHTS** offer the basics to biblical interpretation:

L – Literal Principle
I – Illumination by the Holy Spirit Principle
G – Grammatical Principle
H – Historical Principle
T – Typological Principle
S – Scriptural Harmony Principle

Principles of Biblical Interpretation: **LIGHTS**[1]

1. **Literal Principle**: The Bible must be read literally until we are otherwise forced to understand the passage in question figuratively (Jn 6: 63; 10:7).

2. Illumination Principle (Scripture interprets Scripture): Obscure passages of Scripture must be interpreted in light of clearer passages of Scripture. Only the Holy Spirit can illuminate the truth of the text so that the believer can understand the meaning by faith.

[1] Hank Hanegraaff, The Apocalypse Code, x.

(i). Everything that is essential to salvation and Christian living is clearing revealed in Scripture. There is no essential truth that is hidden away somewhere in the text.

(ii). Illumination is necessary because man's mind has been darkened through sin (Rom 1:21), preventing him from properly understanding God's Word. Human beings cannot understand God's Word apart from God's divine power (Eph 4:18).

Example: 1 Cor 15: 29 – We cannot build a doctrine of baptizing for the dead based upon this Scripture. It is highly likely that Paul is saying this: "You people in the Church at Corinth who claim that the day of the Lord is past, why do you practice proxy-baptism which presumes that the day of the Lord has not come?

3. Good and Necessary Inference Principle: An inference is a fact reasonably implied from another fact. It is a logical consequence. The interpreter derives a conclusion from a given fact or premise. It is the deduction of one proposition from another proposition. Such inferential facts or propositions are sufficiently binding when their truth is established by competent and satisfactory evidence.

Example: MT 22:23-33 And as for the resurrection of the dead, have you not what was said to you by God: **I am** the God of Abraham, and the God of Isaac, and the God of Jacob? He is not God of the dead, but of the living. Jesus refers the Sadducees to Ex 3:6 to show that he is the God of Abraham and not he was the God of Abraham. In John 8:48, Jesus tells the Pharisees, "unless you believe that I AMyou will die in your sins."[2]

4. Historical-Grammatical Principle. The Bible is best understood when one is familiar with the customs, culture, and historical setting of biblical times. Additionally, the interpreter must understand the Bible grammatically before he can understand it theologically. The Bible consists of divine words that must be interpreted in their context.

Example 1: 1 Cor 8:5 For although there may be so-called gods in heaven or on earth—as indeed there are many "gods" and many "lords" yet for us there is one God, the Father, from whom are all things and for whom we exist, and one Lord, Jesus Christ, through whom are all things and through whom we exist.

(i) Mormons have traditionally used this verse as a "proof text" to teach polytheism. However, a simple reading of the whole verse in the context of the whole chapter (e.g. where Paul calls these gods "so-called"), plainly demonstrates that Paul is not teaching polytheism. In order to understand the biblical author's intended meaning, the exegete must interpret the verse in its context.

Example 2: John 1:1 In the beginning was the Word, and the Word was with God, and the Word was God.

Ἐν ἀρχῇ ἦν ὁ λόγος, καὶ ὁ λόγος ἦν πρὸς τὸν θεόν, καὶ θεὸς ἦν ὁ λόγος.

[2] **ἐγώ εἰμί** Ego Eimi, I AM, Jesus claimed to be co-equal and co-eternal with God the Father.

En arche ehn ha Logos kai ha Logos ehn pros ton Theon kai Theos ehn ha Logos.

In (the) beginning was the Word and the Word was with God and God was the Word.

(ii) Word order in Greek is flexible and is used for emphasis. We know the "the Word" is the subject because it has the definite article ὁ (Ha), and therefore we translate it "and the Word was God."

(iii) The word "God" θεὸς (Theos) lacks the definite article, and because of that it keeps us from identifying Person of the Word (Jesus Christ) with the Person of God (The Father). The word order tells us that Jesus Christ has all the divine attributes that the Father has, and the lack of the definite article tells us that Jesus Christ is not the Father.

(iv) To state this another way, look at how the different Greek constructions would be rendered:

καὶ ὁ λόγος ἦν ὁ θεὸς "and the Word was the God" (the Word was the Father) = Sabellianism

καὶ ὁ λόγος ἦν θεὸς "and the Word was a god" = Arianism (Jehovah's Witnesses

καὶ θεὸς ἦν ὁ λόγος " and the Word was God" = Orthodoxy

(v) Jesus Christ is God and has all the attributes that the Father has, but he is not the Father or the Holy Spirit.[3]

5. Typological Principle (Progressive Revelation). The new is in the old concealed; the old is in the new revealed.

Example: In Paul's Epistle to the Galatians, the period before Christ is designated as a period of childhood, tutelage, immaturity, grammar school education. In the fullness of time Christ came and with him comes the full revelation with its maturity of doctrine and morality. This does not imply that the OT is less inspired. This principle states that we must view the OT through the lens of the New Testament and not vice versa.

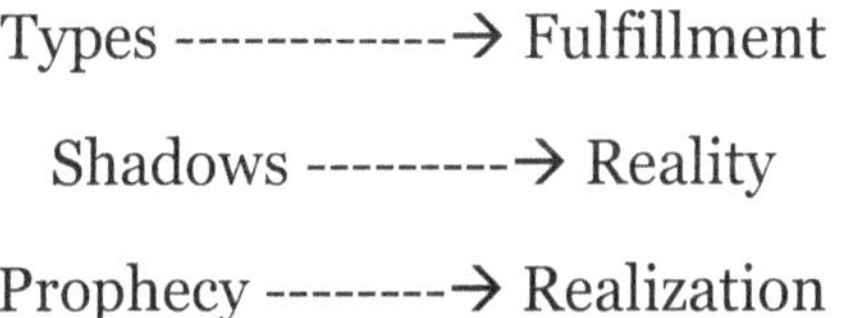

6. Scripture Harmony Principle (The Analogy of Faith). There is one system of truth contained in Scripture, and therefore Scripture does not contradict Scripture. This is also known as the harmony of Scripture rule.

Example: Kopher, kippurim, and kapporeth are translated ransom, redemption, and atonement, "Mercy-seat." They are all derived from the root wood kaphar, which means "to cover." This contains the idea

[3] William Mounce, Basics of Biblical Grammar, 27-28.

of a redemption or atonement brought about by a certain covering.

(i) Also, the New Testament word ἐκκλησία[4] ekklesia, derived from ek and kalein. It is a designation of the Church and points to the fact that the Church consists of people that are "called out" (Mt 16:18, 18:17; Acts 11:22, 12:1,5, etc.).

Gordon Fee's Basic Rules of Exegesis

1: Survey the historical context in general.
2: Confirm the limits of the passage.
3: Become thoroughly acquainted with your paragraph or pericope.
4: Analyze sentence structures and syntactical relationships.
5: Establish the text.
6: Analyze the grammar.
7: Analyze significant words.
8: Research the historical-cultural background.

Granville Sharp's Rule for Demonstrating the Deity of Christ

Statement of the rule: When two personal nouns of the same case are connected by the copulative καὶ (kai), if the former has the definitive article, and the latter has not, they both relate to the same person. This rule is very important in translating and understanding of

---

[4] **ἐκκλησία** (ekklesia)1577, people *called out from* the world to God, the *outcome* being the *Church* (the mystical *body of Christ*) – i.e. the universal (total) body of believers whom God calls *out* from the world and *into* His eternal kingdom.

such passages as Titus 2:13 and 2 Peter 1:1 (as well as others), and as these passages bear directly on the discussion of the Deity of the Lord Jesus Christ.

Example 1: Titus 2:13 "waiting for our blessed hope, the appearing of our great God and Savior Jesus Christ."

ἐπιφάνειαν τῆς δόξης τοῦ μεγάλου θεοῦ καὶ σωτῆρος ἡμῶν Χριστοῦ Ἰησοῦ,

ephiphanean tes doxes tou megalou Theou **kai** soteros hemon Christou Iehsou.

The appearing of the glory of the great God **and** Savior of us Christ Jesus.

Example 2: 2 Peter 1:1 "by the righteous of our God and Savior Jesus Christ:"

ἐν δικαιοσύνῃ τοῦ θεοῦ ἡμῶν καὶ σωτῆ ρος Ἰησοῦ Χριστοῦ,

ehn dikaiahsuneh tou Theou hemon **kai** sotereos Iehsou Christou.

by the righteousness of the God of us **and** Savior Jesus Christ.

Some have simply by-passed grammatical rules and considerations, and have decided for an inferior translation on the basis of verse 2, which, they say, "clearly distinguishes" between God and Christ. The Epistle of Second Peter contains a total of five "Granville Sharp" constructions. They are **1:1**, **1:11**, **2:20**, **3:2**, and **3:18**. No one would argue that the other four instances are exceptions to the rule. For example, in 2:20, it is obvious that both "Lord" and "Savior" are in reference to Christ. Such is the case in 3:2, as well as 3:18.[5]

ἀπεκρίθη Θωμᾶς καὶ εἶπεν αὐτῷ· ὁ κύριος μου καὶ ὁ θεός μου!

Apekreeheh Thomas kai ehpen auto ha Kupios moo kai ha Theos moo!

Answered Thomas and said to him the Lord of me and the God of me!

Dr. A. T. Robertson examined this very subject, and in conclusion said, Sharp stands vindicated after all the dust has settled. We must let these passages mean what they want to mean regardless of our theories about the theology of the writers.[6]

---

[5] James White, Alpha and Omega Ministries.

[6] A. T. Robertson, A Grammar of the Greek New Testament in the Light of Historical Research, pp. 786-787.

Conclusion

"Expect great things from God, attempt great things for God." – William Carey

The greatest honor any man can have is the opportunity to serve the Lord as His undershepherd. Full commitment to this great honor exacts a high price – everything. David supplies the words for this pastoral mindset: "I will not offer to the Lord that which costs me nothing" (2 Sam 24:24). What we find is, service itself is its own reward. And God's people deserve the very best we can offer (Acts 20:28).

The God-given role of a pastor is to serve the Lord Jesus as His undershepherd by: Guiding, providing and protecting Christ's sheep. In conclusion to all that has been said, I offer these final thoughts which constitute five core values. It is my prayer that these values will keep you focused as you serve in your assigned plot of God's vineyard:

1. Commitment to Biblical Truth – Commit to biblical truth and affirm historic, evangelical Christianity. This is a commitment to the inerrancy of Scripture in all its parts (2 Tim 3:16-17). Everything we need to know and believe about God, the world and ourselves is clearly revealed in the Bible. If you don't stand for the inerrancy of the Scripture, you will fall for anything.

2. Be Totally Dependent on God – Be totally dependent on God for the provision of all your needs. As John Owen has rightly observed, "To suppose that whatever God requires of us that we have power of ourselves to do, is to make the cross and grace of Jesus Christ of none effect." God invests His purpose in leaders who are weak and imperfect, so that in victory, His glory is more clearly displayed (Is 40:29-31; 2 Cor 12:9). Never attempt to do the Lord's work in your own strength. Go forth in God's strength, not your own.

3. Be a Man of Prayer – Commit to be a man of prayer. Prayer is foundational to your life and ministry. James I. Packer rightly said, "What we do every time we pray is to confess our impotence and God's sovereignty." By prayer you can seek God's direction, request resources, and call upon the Holy Spirit to empower our ministry (Rom 8:26-27).

4. Be Christ-Centered – Strive to glorify Christ in all that you do. Strive to become like Christ in love, servanthood, holiness, and obedience to the Father. Follow Christ's example in sacrifice, hardship and even death (Rom 8:16-17). Christ is all, all for Christ!

5. Be Mission-Focused – Be committed to the urgent and unfinished task of making disciples of Jesus Christ in all nations (Mt 28:18-20). Make disciples who will make disciples. Work with others and churches who share this vision. "And this gospel of the kingdom will be preached in all the world as a witness to all the nations, and then the end will come" (Mt 24:14). As George Whitefield said, "We are immortal till our work is done."

Godspeed.

About the Author

Paul D. LeFavor was born in Virginia and was raised in a pastor's family. He graduated from Liberty University and received his M.A. in Religion from Reformed Theological Seminary and his M.Div. from Liberty Theological Seminary. Paul retired from the US Army Special Forces in 2009, is married to Becky, his wife of twenty-four years, and has two daughters Liane and Collette. He has served as the pastor of Christ Covenant Baptist Church, Fayetteville, North Carolina since 2012 and is the author of five books.

Hebrew Alphabet

א – Aleph
ב – Beth
ג – Gemel
ד – Daleth
ה – He
ו – Waw
ז – Zayin
ח – Heth
ט – Teth
י – Yod
כ – Kaph
ל – Lamed
מ – Mem
נ – Nun
ס – Samek
ע – Ayin
פ – Pe
צ – Tsadde
ק – Qoph
ר – Resh
ש – Shin
ת – Tau

Greek Alphabet

Α α – Alpha
Β β – Beta
Γ γ – Gamma
Δ δ – Delta
Ε ε – Epsilon
Ζ ζ – Zeta
Η η – Eta
Θ θ – Theta
Ι ι – Iota
Κ κ – Kappa
Λ λ – Lambda
Μ μ – Mu
Ν ν – Nu
Ξ ξ – Xi
Ο ο – Omicron
Π π – Pi
Ρ ρ – Rho
Σ σ/ς, – Sigma
Τ τ – Tau
Υ υ – Upsilon
Φ φ – Phi
Χ χ – Chi
Ψ ψ – Psi
Ω ω – Omega

Vocabulary Words

(*English – Greek*)

All – πᾶς, πᾶσα, πᾶν
And – καί
Angel – ἄγγελος
Announce – ἀπαγγέλλω
Anointing – χρίσμα
Authority – ἐξουσία
Bad – κακός
Baptize – βαπτίζω
Beginning – ἀρχή
Believe – πιστεύω
Beloved – ἀγαπητός
Bless – εὐλογέω
Blessed – μακάριος
Blood – αἷμα
Body – σῶμα
Book – βιβλίον
Bread – ἄρτος
Brother – ἀδελφός
Call – καλέω
Child – τέκνον
Christ – Χριστός
Church – ἐκκλησία
City – πόλις
Cleanse – καθαρίζω
Come – ἔρχομαι
Comfort – παρακαλέω
Comforter – παράκλητος
Commandment – ἐντολή
Confess – ὁμολογέω
Conquer – νικάω
Crucify – σταυρόω
Darkness – σκότος
Daughter – θυγάτηρ
Day – ἡμέρα
Dead – νεκρός
Death – θάνατος
Deceive – πλανάω
Demon – δαίμων
Deny – ἀρνέομαι
Desire – ἐπιθυμία
Destroy – φθείρω
Die – ἀποθνῄσκω
Disciple – μαθητής
Do – ποιέω
Down – κατά
Draw near – ἐγγίζω
Drink – πίνω
Ear – οὖς
Eat – ἐσθίω
End – τέλος

Evil – πονηρός
Eye – ὀφθαλμός
Faith – πίστις
Faithful – πιστός
Fall – πίπτω
Father – πατήρ
Fellowship – κοινωνία
First – πρῶτος
Fish – ἰχθύς
Fisherman – ἁλιεύς
Flesh – σάρξ
Forgive – ἀφίημι
From – από, ἐκ
Fruit – καρπός
Gentiles – ἔθνος
Gift – δῶρον
Give – δίδωμι
Give thanks – εὐχαριστέω
Glorify – δοξάζω
Go – ἔρχομαι
God – θεός
Good – ἀγαθός
Gospel – εὐαγγέλιον
Grace – χάρισ
Great – μέγας
Hand – χειρ
Hate – μισέω
Have – ἔχω
Heal – ἰάομαι, θεραπεύω
Heart – καρδία
Heaven – οὐρανός
Hell – ᾍδης
Holy Spirit – πνεύματος ἁγίου
Hope – ἐλπίς
I – ἐγώ
If – ἐάν
In – ἐν
In order that – ἵνα
Instead of – ἀντί, ὑπέρ
Into – εἰσ
Jesus – Ἰησοῦς
Joy – χαρά
Judge – κρίνω
Judgment – κρίσις
Just – δίκαιος
Kill – ἀποκτείνω
King – βασιλεύς
Kingdom – βασιλεία
Know – γινώσκω
Knowledge – γνῶσις
Language – γλῶσσα
Last – ἔσχατος
Law – νομος
Lead – ἄγω
Lie – ψεῦδος, ψεύδομαι
Life – βίος, ζωή

Light – φῶς
Lord – κύριος
Love – ἀγάπη
Lust – ἐπιθυμία
Man – ἄνθρωπος
Marriage – γάμος
Mercy – ἔλεος
Messenger – ἄγγελος
Mother – μήτηρ
Mountain – ὄρος
Mouth – στόμα
Much – πολύς
Name – ὄνομα
Nation – ἔθνος
New – καινός
Offense – σκάνδαλον
Old – παλαιός
Only – μόνος
Other – ἕτερος
Our – ἡμᾶς
Peace – εἰρήνη
People – λαός
Perfect – τελειόω
Power – δύναμις
Praise – δόξα
Pray – προσεύχομαι
Preach – κηρύσσω
Preacher – κῆρυξ
Prepare – ἑτοιμάζω
Presence – παρουσία
Priest – ἱερεύς
Promise – ἐπαγγελία
Prophet – προφήτης
Propitiation – ἱλασμός
Purify – καθαρίζω
Raise up – ἐγείρω
Receive – λαμβάνω
Remain – μένω
Resurrection – ἀνάστασις
Righteous – δίκαιος
Righteousness –δικαιοσύνη
Sacred – ἅγιος
Salvation – σωτηρία
Sanctify – ἁγιάζω
Save – σῴζω
Scripture – γραφή
Sea – θάλασσα
See – βλέπω
Servant – διάκονος
Sin – ἁμαρτία
Slave – δοῦλος
Son – υἱός
Spirit – πνεῦμα
Teach – διδάσκω
Temple – ἱερόν
Water – ὕδωρ
Witness – μάρτυς
Word – λόγος

Recommended Reading List

1. Adams, Jay E. *Shepherding God's Flock.*
2. Augustine, *Confessions.*
3. Baxter, Richard *The Godly Home.*
4. Beale, Greg *The Temple and the Church's Mission.*
5. Bisagno, John *Pastor's Handbook*
6. Boice, James *Foundations of the Christian Faith.*
7. Bonhoeffer, Dietrich *The Cost of Discipleship.*
8. Bunyan, John *Pilgrims Progress.*
9. Bunyan, John *The Holy War.*
10. Calvin, John *Institutes of the Christian Religion.*
11. Carson, D.A. *How Long, O Lord?*
12. Clowney, Edmund *The Church.*
13. Edwards, Jonathan *Religious Affections.*
14. Lewis, C.S. *Mere Christianity.*
15. Lewis, C.S. *The Problem of Pain.*
16. Lewis, C.S. *The Screwtape Letters.*
17. Lloyd-Jones, David M. *Preaching and Preachers.*
18. MacArthur, John *The Master's Plan for the Church.*
19. MacArthur, John *Pastoral Ministry.*
20. Packer, J.I. *Evangelism and the Sovereignty of God.*
21. Packer, J.I. *God's Words.*
22. Packer, J.I. *Knowing God.*
23. Piper, John *Let the Nations be Glad.*
24. Piper, John *What Jesus Demands from the World.*
25. Prime, Derek and Begg, Alistair *On Being a Pastor.*
26. Ryle, J.C. *Thoughts for Young Men.*
27. Sanders, J. Oswald *Spiritual Leadership.*
28. Sproul, R.C. *The Last Days According to Jesus.*
29. Spurgeon, Charles H. *Lectures to My Students.*
30. Wells, David F. *God in the Wasteland.*

Scripture Index

www.ingramcontent.com/pod-product-compliance
Lightning Source LLC
Chambersburg PA
CBHW020248030426
42336CB00010B/663
* 9 7 8 1 7 3 2 9 6 8 1 3 4 *